Jan. 2016

Dear Paul,

Many thanks for constructive comments and suggestions at the Rosendal conference!
Best

Fleur, Rune, & Knut

After the Mass Party

After the Mass Party

Continuity and Change in Political Parties and Representation in Norway

Elin Haugsgjerd Allern, Knut Heidar, and Rune Karlsen

LEXINGTON BOOKS
Lanham • Boulder • New York • London

Published by Lexington Books
An imprint of The Rowman & Littlefield Publishing Group, Inc.
4501 Forbes Boulevard, Suite 200, Lanham, Maryland 20706
www.rowman.com

Unit A, Whitacre Mews, 26-34 Stannary Street, London SE11 4AB

British Library Cataloguing in Publication Information Available

Library of Congress Cataloging-in-Publication Data

Allern, Elin Haugsgjerd.
  After the mass party : continuity and change in political parties and representation in Norway / Elin Haugsgjerd Allern, Knut Heidar, and Rune Karlsen.
    pages cm
  Includes bibliographical references and index.
  ISBN 978-1-4985-1654-9 (cloth : alk. paper) – ISBN 978-1-4985-1655-6 (ebook)
  1. Political parties–Norway. 2. Representative government and representation–Norway.
  I. Heidar, Knut, 1949- II. Karlsen, Rune. III. Title.
    JN7691.A1A55 2016
    324.2481–dc23
                                    2015033457

Printed in the United States of America

To the memory of
Hanne Marthe Narud (1958–2012)

Contents

List of Figures

List of Tables

Preface and Acknowledgments

This book started with a research group established by means of a grant from the Norwegian Research Council (NRC) from 2009 to 2012 ("Political Parties and Democracy: Decline or Change?" project number 185436). The aim was to contribute to the debate on the consequences of declining mass membership parties for the role of parties in contemporary democracies. The strategy was to bring together scholars from both the party organization and the electoral-parliamentary fields of research in a unified, comprehensive approach.

Hanne Marthe Narud was the leader of the project which also included Elin Haugsgjerd Allern and Knut Heidar. Rune Karlsen and Anders Ravik Jupskås were later brought in to strengthen and extend project capacities. Anders, as PhD fellow, took care of all practical aspects of the 2009 party member and delegate surveys. This was no minor task: As many as 8,800 questionnaires were distributed and field work at seven different party congresses was carried out.

The plan was to pursue several semi-independent research projects under one umbrella, with the clear intention of adding much of it up to one overarching monograph in the end. Sadly, Hanne Marthe was not able to take part in this final book project as she became seriously ill and died in July 2012. Her untimely death deprived her of the opportunity to execute the great ideas she had for the final project output. We are deeply sorry we could not share the challenges and joys of writing this book with Hanne Marthe.

We have worked on the book since the spring of 2012. It has taken time, not only because of the difficult start and the extensive work necessary, but also due to several "parallel projects and obligations." In due course, we have accumulated many debts to institutions and individuals who, in one way or another, have helped us in addition to the NRC. In the spring of 2013 we presented a preliminary draft at a project conference in Rosendal, on the west coast of Norway, to a group of international specialists. We are very thankful to Thomas Poguntke, Jo Saglie, Lars Svåsand, Jacques Thomassen, and Paul Webb for taking the time and for offering constructive critique and useful advice. Their input provided valuable guidance for our work. We would also like to thank Kaare Strøm for commenting on a later version which also led to substantial revisions. Helpful feedback has in addition been received on papers presented at the following events: the IPSA World Congress in Madrid in 2012, a conference on party membership at the University of Copenhagen in June 2013, the ECPR General Conference in Bordeaux in 2013, at the ECPR Joint Sessions in Salamanca in 2014, and at the weekly research seminars of the Department of Political Science at the University of Oslo. Anonymous reviews from the publisher gave us constructive comments enabling us to tighten up and clarify the text. Moreover, we would like to express gratitude to Lexington Books' editors—Justin Race, Joseph Parry, Sarah Craig, and Emily Roderick—for their support during the entire publication and production process. The result as presented here, however, is of course our own responsibility.

The analyses could not have been completed without the openness of the Norwegian political parties. We are grateful for the party leaderships' support when distributing surveys to party members, congress delegates, and members of parliament at the beginning of the project. We would also like to thank all the party affiliates and officials who filled out the questionnaires despite a busy schedule during an election year. The same goes for the sample of voters who responded to a long list of questions as well.

The Norwegian Election Study (NES), under the long-standing leadership of the late Henry Valen and Bernt Aardal, certainly deserves a tribute. The NES-time series have been essential to our project. We have also used data from many other sources in order to describe voters, parliamentarians, and electoral candidates—and the party context—which are noted in the text.

During the entire process we have enjoyed excellent working conditions at the Department of Political Science, University of Oslo, and at different stages the project at large has benefited from visiting fellowships at the University of Sussex (UK) and the University of Auckland (New Zealand).

A warm thank you goes out to Peder Wahl, secretary for the book project *The History of the Storting 1964–2014* (*Stortingets historie 1964–2014*), for aid with collecting financial data. Last, but not least, we would like to acknowledge the help of a number of clever student assistants in Oslo. The following have contributed to the data collection, in the processing of tables and figures, and/or in handling the manuscript towards the end (in alphabetical order): Jannicke Fredriksen, Eirik Hildal, Anne Høyer, Maiken Røed, Torill Stavenes, and Jonas Tysland.

We dedicate this book to the memory of Hanne Marthe Narud—distinguished researcher, organizer, colleague, and friend. *After the Mass Party* would not have been written without her.

Elin Haugsgjerd Allern, Knut Heidar, and Rune Karlsen

List of Abbreviations

Parties	English name	Norwegian name
ALP/FrP	Progress Party	Fremskrittspartiet
Ap	Labour Party	Arbeiderpartiet
H	Conservatives (Conservative Party)	Høyre
KrF	Christian People's Party	Kristelig Folkeparti
Sp	Centre Party	Senterpartiet
SV	Socialist Left Party	Sosialistisk Venstreparti
V	Liberals (Liberal Party)	Venstre

1

Political Parties and Representative Democracy

In most established parliamentary democracies, parties have lost members, and they increasingly rely on state subventions to finance their activities. Their ties to civil society are weaker than those of the "mass parties" operating after WWII. The message in much recent research, particularly on European parties, is that these changes threaten party-based democracy: today, parties rule more than they represent (e.g., Katz and Mair 1995; 2009; van Biezen, Mair, and Poguntke 2012; Mair 2006; 2013). In this book, we test this argument by examining the extent to which parties' representative capacity has in fact declined in the wake of their decay as membership organizations. Has parties' ability to channel voter interests into political institutions weakened since the heyday of mass parties?

We question both the theoretical and empirical foundations of the decline thesis. First, we argue that one needs to better specify what party-based representation through membership organizations means, and that we must examine the conditions under which fewer members and more state financing is likely to result in a decline in party representation. Second, we contend that there has not been enough empirical research to substantiate claims of decline, partly due to a lack of appropriate data.

Accordingly, this book has a dual purpose. First, we aim to critically discuss *why* one should expect a decline in parties' membership organization to weaken party representation. We argue that this brings up an essential question in modern democracies: whether the organizational party channel is significant or irrelevant, given the representative capacity parties generate through the electoral channel. The distinction is also familiar in the US–European divide in evaluating the role of parties in democracy (e.g., Ranney 1951; Wright 1971). Second, on this basis, we make two empirical enquiries by looking at the viability of members' intra-party activities and the degree to which voters' social backgrounds and political attitudes match the social profile and policy views of the party members, party organizational elites, and parliamentary representatives. First, we examine relevant empirical studies both of voters and party organizations (members and activists), and of voters and parliamentary groups (members of parliaments, MPs) to summarize what we already know. Second, we present an in-depth case study of Norwegian voters and parties, based on a number of longitudinal surveys conducted between 1990 and 2010.

Finally, in the last chapter, we summarize our main findings. We conclude that the comparative, empirical literature is scarce and indecisive, whereas the Norwegian parties still seem to represent voters fairly well, both socially and on important policy issues, despite the waning of mass parties. We argue that the high policy congruence between voters and parties (members of parliament) in Norway, which has remained stable, might be related to the fact that party members and mid-level activists still resemble voters on important social and political variables to a large degree.

At the same time, the party competition for votes still is relatively efficient, and there appears to be some interaction in terms of what happens within party organizations and the stimuli offered by competing parties. We conclude by discussing what might explain the patterns of stability and change revealed in the study, and we offer some ideas for future work on party change and its impact in contemporary representative democracies. We argue that similar patterns might be expected to appear beyond Norway as well, while noting that persistence of the mass parties' formal representative structures, and Norway's closed candidate selection processes, perhaps make Norwegian parties somewhat more resistant to shifting toward a widening gap between voters and parties.

THE RISE AND DECLINE OF THE MASS PARTY

The "mass party" model first referred to the socialist membership parties that emerged outside the national assemblies, based on trade union movements, cooperatives, and friendly societies (Duverger [1954] 1972, 17, 24–27, 75ff.). Party organization was a tool for a rising working class that lacked political rights, financial resources, and actual influence. Its fundamental unit was the branch and its members (ibid., 25, 63). Catholic parties and agrarian parties adopted similar structures when organizing religious groups and farmers (Duverger [1954] 1972, 6). The bourgeois parties, in contrast, primarily represented the upper classes, and normally began with sufficient financial resources and easy access to public office. However, in systems with universal suffrage, these cadre parties had to follow the example of the mass parties if they were to retain their influence over time (Duverger [1954] 1972, xxvii). In the early 1950s, when Duverger published the first edition of his book, non-left parties were trying to incorporate their supporters into formal organizations (Scarrow 2002; 2015). He predicted that liberal and conservative parties alike would adapt to the mass party model to maintain electoral support.

In the beginning, the role of mass parties in democracy was hotly debated. Scholars like Mosei Ostrogorski (1902) generally feared that well-organized parties would destroy democracy by introducing a regimentation of opinions that would curb free deliberation among "the best men." Robert Michels (1911) saw mass parties as emerging oligarchies with no potential to provide democracy. Gradually, however, parties with a large membership and intra-party democracy became a normative ideal among Europe-oriented party scholars (Duverger 1954; Assarson 1993; Katz and Mair 1995). It was argued that such parties opened up the possibility of grassroots participation, educating the mass electorate in responsible citizenship and, consequently, strengthening the linkage between voters and representatives in public office (Heidar 2006; Allern and Pedersen 2007).

What happens, then, when these parties start to decline as membership organizations, and the state takes over as their financial provider? It has long been argued that social, technological, cultural, and political developments have made the mass party model outdated (Kirchheimer 1966). As early as in 1954, Otto Kirchheimer introduced the concept of the *catch-all party.* In his view, major West German parties no longer fitted the mass party model in terms of presenting a clear and overarching class- or group-based policy to their voters. Instead, they emphasized a "brokerage role" by seeking support from among numerous segments. The personalities and qualities of party leaders dominated media appeals, and a more "catch-all" approach to electoral campaigning indicated weakening ties to specific social classes (Kirchheimer 1966, 186). Parties were changing from mass-based into elite-dominated, professional parties.

Some thirty years later, Katz and Mair (1995) argued that "the sheer size and commitment of party memberships have generally failed to keep pace with the growth in electorates, on the one hand, and with the rapid escalating costs of party activity, on the other" (15). Parties had to look elsewhere for resources. Members were less useful to party leaders due to new means of communication (21). Parties became more elite-driven, dominated by parliamentary groups. They expected the transformation of catch-all parties into yet another organizational form: the *cartel party* (Katz and Mair 1995; 2009).

Another systemic trend supported these changes: party competition took on the characteristics of an oligopolistic market more strongly. State subventions became a major financial resource for established parties and created barriers to emergent ones (Katz and Mair 1995, 15). Given the absence of great policy battles in recent decades, winning or losing made less of a difference in parties' political objectives. Hence, the conditions had become ideal for the formation of a cartel. The result was—in effect—interparty collusion (Katz and Mair 1995, 22; Pelizzo 2003, 40), as Kirchheimer had already foreseen in the early 1960s. Within a cartelized party system, parties developed professional organizations that were weakly rooted in civil society and characterized by closeness to the state (Katz and Mair 1995, 23). Thus, with the advent of "cartel parties," not only was the era of party membership organizations over, but party competition for votes had also become more limited. The declining need for party members and their services, combined with decreasing party competition in the electoral markets, seems, therefore, to be the central force behind the rise of the cartel party.

The extent to which "catch-all parties," "cartel parties," and, not least, "cartelized" party systems actually exist is disputed (Katz and Mair 2009). It is, however, widely agreed that the era of the mass membership party is over. Undoubtedly, over the past three decades, party membership in most countries has declined significantly (van Biezen, Mair, and Poguntke 2012; Scarrow 2015). Party elites have become more powerful at the expense of ordinary party members. Parties have become increasingly centralized due to external changes, like the "medialization of politics," the personalization of political communication, and state financing (Katz 2013, 63). At the same time, there is also a trend of granting participatory rights to registered supporters and non-members. Scarrow (2015) shows that parties now offer members better opportunities to participate in party decisions. They also offer new, lower-cost modes of party affiliation by means of new information technology. These changes may promote party legitimacy among the broader public. Some argue, however, that granting more formal rights to rank-and-file members weakens the party stratum that might actually exert influence and keep party leadership accountable: mid-level activists (Katz and Mair 1995).

There are also clear indications of a loosening of the old strong, stable ties between the former mass parties and their electorates. Parties' grip on voters is waning. Decreasing party identification and increasing electoral volatility are well documented (Dalton 2000; Dalton, McAllister, and Wattenberg 2000). In recent decades, the public has increasingly turned to various types of interest groups and ad-hoc protests—including more individualistic modes of action, like signing petitions—to make its voice heard (Dalton 2006). The major campaign arena is not found at conventions, rallies, or caucuses, but rather in newspapers, on the national radio, on TV, and on the Internet (Farrell and Webb 2000).

A common first reaction to these developments was that parties' general contribution to democracy's well-being was at stake (e.g., Lawson and Merkl 1988). As the pool of active citizens became smaller, the consequence of party membership decline was weaker democracy, it was argued (van der Meer and van Ingen 2009; Whiteley 2009, 137). Even more scholars have reasoned that the *way* parties function within democracy has *changed*: they have declined as channels for popular demands and as facilitators of citizen control over MPs and other public representatives (Kirchheimer 1966; Dalton and Wattenberg 2000; Webb 2000; Strøm, Müller, and Bergman 2003; van Biezen 2004a; Voerman and van Schuur 2011; Whiteley 2011). Some claim that the parties have lost their legitimacy as representative organizations. Parties had withdrawn from civil society and turned into semi-state agencies, or "public utilities" (Katz and Mair 1995; van Biezen 2004b). Parties were "failing" as "citizens retreat[ed] into private life . . . while party leaderships retreat[ed] into institutions" (Mair 2006, 11). This signaled a "democracy that . . . [was] being steadily stripped of its popular component—democracy without a demos" (ibid., 1).

A less bold and more widespread claim is that a shift has taken place from the *combined* representative ("input") and procedural ("output") roles of parties to a more exclusively procedural function, in terms of recruitment, organization of government, and delivery of public policies (e.g., Bartolini and Mair 2001, 336). As the party in the public office still appears strong, the decay of parties as membership organizations primarily has weakened parties' ability to provide citizen mobilization and the aggregation or representation of voter preferences (Ignazi 1996; Strøm and Svåsand 1997; Allern and Pedersen 2007).

Consequently, according to van Biezen, Mair, and Poguntke (2012), the parties' grassroot members today have more in common with the elite than with the electorate: "It might be reasonable to regard them not as constituting part of civil society—with which party membership has traditionally been associated—but rather as constituting the outer ring of an extended political class" (van Biezen, Mair, and Poguntke 2012, 39). With these words, they revisit Ostrogorski's old claim that party organizations were unrepresentative of voters in general ([1902] 1964). But while Ostrogorski argued that this trait was intrinsic to party organizations, contemporary party scholars tend to argue that the representative capacity of organized parties declined with the decline of the mass party. In short, the decline of the mass party is argued to have increased the overall social and political "distance" between voters and national party elites. The boldest version of this argument implies greater differences between voters and parties in general, not only between individual parties and their voters.

Overall, these arguments reflect the status of the mass party as the normative ideal in Europe, but as we will show in chapter 3, the jury is still out on the question of whether the representative capacity of parties has actually declined. Clearly, there is both insufficient and mixed empirical evidence. Moreover, it is necessary to specify the conditions under which weakened mass parties are likely to result in less representative party organizations and when less representative organizations will affect parties' representative capacity in the public office. A basic assumption seems to be that parties with declining membership will attract a different kind of party activist, one who will make it more likely that the party organization will select candidates and policies that alienate party supporters. If the pool of potential party candidates changes, the social and political profiles of candidates and, eventually, elected MPs may change as well. However, having fewer and less financially important members does not necessarily mean having disempowered, less representative members.

KEY RESEARCH QUESTION

All too often we are willing to accept claims that are frequently repeated, even before the facts are presented. The decline of parties' ability to channel the demands of voters to elected representatives is about to become one of these "facts." The present book makes a serious attempt to check whether this is actually true, or if it is more of a myth. Parties are not like they once were and changes in the way they work seem inevitable. Undoubtedly, they mobilize fewer citizens than before and they are increasingly financed by the state across countries. But does this weakened capacity to *recruit and engage* really affect their ability to *represent* voters? In this book we address this question by concentrating on the party members, activists, and MPs. For the issue of representation the individuals entitled to shape party decisions are obviously relevant targets of analysis and the use of aggregated survey data enables direct comparison of voters' and parties' positions. Consequently, the formal structures of parties—an important part of former mass parties that has also significantly changed in some polities (Kirchheimer 1966; Katz and Mair 1995)—are seen as one of the factors that might impinge on the relationship.

In line with Hanna Pitkin (1967), in chapter 2, we define "representation" as "acting in the interest of the represented, in a manner responsive to them" (209). We discuss this core concept and potential measurements, and argue that a high degree of congruence between voters and the different party layers in terms of their social background and policy views indicates high representative capacity, while low congruence indicates low representative capacity. We also argue that for party affiliates outside parliament to matter, they need to be capable of influencing their parties. Accordingly, the primary general research question of this book is: *Have parties' representative capacity—in terms of member activity, communication and influence, and social and political representativeness across various party levels—weakened since the 1970s?*

Analytically, then, we look at both social and issue congruence between voters, on the one hand, and party members, congress delegates, and MPs, on the other. Empirically, we first review a wide body of relevant studies on voters, party members, and MPs along all these dimensions. Research on activities, decision-making processes, and congruence within the party organization is surveyed in light of the framework developed in chapter 2. Second, we examine new longitudinal data (1990–2010) from Norway, consisting of surveys that enable us to examine the developments in one country in detail. Most factors predicting the decline of mass parties were present in Norway during the period examined, including rising educational levels, increased social and geographical mobility, weakened political cleavages, a more individualistic culture, and professional media. Since the 1980s, party membership in Norway has more than halved, and public financial support to parties has increased substantially. All this makes Norway a suitable case for studying the representative capacity of parties "after the mass party." Together, the "meta-study" and the single-country study will provide a basis for our final assessment of the assumed decline in the representative capacity of political parties. In conclusion, we also discuss what might explain the patterns of stability and the changes that we find over time and across parties.

PLAN OF THE BOOK

In chapter 2, we first summarize how parties came to be seen as an inherent part of modern representative democracy. Second, we discuss the concept of representation, identifying congruence in social backgrounds and, above all, policy views as the essential indicators of representative party capacity. Moreover, we argue that the entire chain—from voters, via party members, to party congress delegates and parliamentarians—should be mapped to review party representativeness. Third, we critically discuss the theoretical foundations of the decline of party representation thesis and identify different ways in which political parties contribute to the representation of voters.

We argue that the debate is rooted in an old, partly normative dispute regarding the importance of party organizations versus party competition in parties' ability to provide representation in public office (e.g., Schattschneider 1942; Duverger [1954] 1972). Few contemporary studies, however, focus explicitly on the relative importance of and the relationship between these two mechanisms. Yet these two perspectives lead to different expectations when it comes to parties' representative capacity in public office today. Assuming both mechanisms might matter in the real world, we argue that the consequence of mass party decline for parties' representative roles is not that easy to predict.

Next, we develop an "analytical map" that allows us to study the development empirically in a more systematic and comprehensive way, with particular emphasis on the organizational channel. Activity, communication, and influence among party members are seen as necessary conditions. For the party organizations and activist members to actually matter, there should be internal party processes (activity, member influence) that sustain linkage inside the party organizations. Without such activity and communication, there is no reason to attribute any weight to the membership organization in the supplementation (or distortion) of party congruence between voters and representatives. Parties would, in that case, be merely professional organizations that help party candidates compete for public office.

In chapter 3, we undertake a "meta-study" of the empirical literature. We conclude that the claim that parties have declined as agencies of representation from the 1980s onward has been neither confirmed nor rejected by existing research. One obvious reason for this is the limited and not very reliable data available on party members; another is that longitudinal data are either non-existent or impressionistic.

The case study of Norway—conducted in the next four chapters—represents our original empirical contribution. In chapter 4, we discuss how much bearing the Norwegian political environment has on the analytical questions raised in the book. How strongly have Norwegian parties, as organizations, been stimulated to "move away" from voters? We also briefly discuss how Norway scores for a few other contextual factors that might directly influence the development of parties' representative capacity in its different guises. Finally, we present the data material to be used in the empirical analysis and discuss its assets and limitations.

In chapters 5–7, we present our main empirical research on Norwegian parties. Both differences between individual Norwegian parties and overall changes are central to the analyses. In chapter 5, we analyze the activity levels, patterns of communication, and influences inside the party organizations. What can party activity at different levels tell us about the abilities of the parties to operate as representative channels? Is there any indication that the organizational layers still "speak" to each other through contacts, debates, and networking, or have the former Norwegian mass parties declined as channels of representation?

In chapters 6 and 7, the development of the representativeness—or "congruence"—of the different party strata and the voters is analyzed. In the former, we study representation as social representation: do MPs, party delegates, and party members differ from voters in terms of age, gender, education, occupation, and income? In the latter, the topic is policy representation: do issue preferences across party levels match, or are there deviations, exceptions, or outright mismatches between voters and members, delegates, and MPs? Moreover, how have the patterns changed over time?

Finally, in the last chapter, chapter 8, we conclude and discuss our findings more generally. If the parties' representative capacity—as measured here—is more or less the same as it once was despite decline in membership, rise in state subsidies, and the huge contextual changes in the structure of political activities in Western democracies, why could that be?

2

Representation by Parties

An Analytical Framework

Why should we expect parties' decline as membership organizations to reduce parties' representative capacity? How we can study these changes empirically? These are the two main questions we address in this chapter. One of the main goals, therefore, is to discuss the concept of representation and critically examine the theoretical foundations of the thesis of the decline of party representation. By investigating the different ways in which parties might serve as instruments for representation, we show that different views on representation lead to different expectations regarding the consequences of mass party decline, and we argue that parties' overall representative capacity depends on member–MP linkage inside the party organization, as well as on the parties' electoral competition for votes. The second main aim is to develop our analytical map of parties' representative capacity and to specify the research questions and measurements used in the empirical analyses. First, however, let us briefly sketch how political parties came to be seen as an essential part of representative democracies.

REPRESENTATIVE DEMOCRACY AND POLITICAL PARTIES

In eighteenth-century debates, democracy was associated with the classic Greek type: direct government in small communities. Leaders were selected for short, limited periods, and were expected to act, not to represent. In Jean-Jacques Rousseau's version of democracy, representation destroyed democracy. Both the protagonists of democracy and advocates of representative government saw democracy and representation as impossible to combine. Nevertheless, modern democracies combine universal suffrage with elected representatives, as this turned out to be the only workable way to practice mass democracy (Manin 1997).

The development of political parties is closely linked to the rise of representative, electoral democracy (Sartori 1976). Parties in their modern form emerged toward the end of the nineteenth century and introduced a stronger organization, more elaborate decision-making processes, and increasingly formalized ties between individuals. Parliamentarians quickly learned that it paid to organize into groups to control and influence the government, as well as to mobilize voters at elections. This power drive triggered a process of negotiation and coordination, which, in essence, led to modern parties.

Parties were widely opposed (and even banned) in the early days (van Biezen 2004a; 2004b; Crotty 2006; Scarrow 2006), but over time, political parties came to be seen as *de facto* inherent to representative democracy (e.g., Bagehot [1867] 2002; Bryce 1921; Schattschneider 1942; Pomper 1992). Democracy today is a representative form of government with principal public officials chosen in free elections, in practice, along some sort of party lines (Katz 1987, 2). That said, there are different views on the general importance of political parties in democracy. According to Wright (1971, 20), a major division developed between the so-called pluralist notion and the majoritarian concept of party-based democracy after WWII.

The first emphasized interest pluralism, and competition between heterogenous interest groups was seen as crucial. Parties should, therefore, not dominate the political system (Epstein 1967, 8; Katz 1997), only "mute conflict by promoting compromise and consensus-building" (Wright 1971, 29). The pluralist position has been advocated by party scholars such as Epstein, Wilson, and Schlesinger, and it is associated with liberal-economic democracy as argued by Schumpeter, Downs, and the American pluralists (like Dahl 1956). The second position, with an emphasis on majority rule, assumes that the parties' main task is to "transmit" this majority's political preferences into public office. To this end, strong parties are necessary (Wright 1971, 23ff.), and interest groups should play a secondary role in the political system. The argument has been predominantly represented by European scholars, like Duverger and Neumann in the party literature, and American scholars within the "responsible parties" tradition, like Schattschneider (1942). "Party government" prevails when parties win control of the executive office through competitive elections, political leaders are recruited by and through the parties, parties offer clear policy alternatives to voters, public policies are determined by the parties holding executive office, and the executive office is held accountable by the voters through the parties (Katz 1987; 1990; Mair 2008, 225).

The tension between these viewpoints still exists, but leading party scholars continue to describe parties as "at the heart" of the political system (Aldrich 2011, 3), "endemic to democracy" (Stokes 1999, 245), etc. Parties interact, at least in Europe, with constitutionally defined groups at every level in the political system: campaigning among voters, organizing local government, selecting candidates for parliament, and providing a basis for the national government, as well as, to varying degrees, influencing the selection of top civil servants. A process of party constitutionalization in post-war Europe consolidated the empirical reality of modern party government (van Biezen 2011). To summarize parties' roles in democracy, the general term "linkage" has been widespread, thanks to Kay Lawson's (e.g., 1980) work, marking parties as "the primary representative agents between citizens and the state" (Dalton, Farrell, and McAllister 2011). The essence of linkage "is the provision of a connection between those in elite positions and the electorate at large" (Poguntke 2002), but the term is also used in another way: as a parallel to the functional roles of parties (e.g., Almond 1960; King 1969; Dalton, Farrell, and McAllister 2011). Our focus is on linkage in the narrow sense: the means or processes that allow political leaders to act in accordance with the public's wants, needs, and demands (Luttbeg 1974, 3).

That said, how parties should organize to make democracy and representation work has been continuously contested. In our view, this long-standing debate can illuminate the contemporary discussion regarding mass party decline and the consequences for parties' representative capacity. However, before examining the various positions, a key question to be addressed is the precise meaning of "representation" and "representative."

THE CONCEPTS OF REPRESENTATION

Hanna Pitkin (1967) argues in her seminal work that representation in democracies implies "a public, institutionalized arrangement involving many people and operating in the complex ways of large scale social arrangements" (221). Etymologically, "representation" means to make "something present which is not in fact present" (Pitkin 1967, 8–9). This definition is reflected in the idea that representative bodies should mirror the people they represent, a concept that implies that representatives do not act for others; they stand for them (Pitkin 1967, 61).

In contemporary terms, the concept of "presence" leads to an emphasis on the social background of representatives and its symbolic value (so-called descriptive representation) (Pitkin 1967; Phillips 1995; Mansbridge 1999). Technically, or statistically, a sample is representative of a population if each member of the population had an equal probability of being chosen for the sample. In political discussion, relevant subgroups are usually groups of a certain age, sex, class, occupation, and racial or ethnic background, that is, groups that either share visible characteristics or experiences in life (Mansbridge 1999, 629). Proponents of presence and descriptive representation believe that social background colors the attitudes and behavior of representatives in one way or another. These characteristics are expected to carry different political interests, even though empirical studies have revealed mixed results on how strong these correlations actually are (Mansbridge 1999; Narud and Valen 2000). Hence, descriptive representation is assumed to lead to substantive representation—that is, to groups being represented in terms of political interests or policy views as well.

Historically, representation has also meant one person acting on behalf of another individual or a group (Pitkin 1967). We find an echo of this usage in contemporary

delegate or "principal–agent" analysis. The agent acts on behalf of and in the principal's interests, with a degree of leeway that varies from case to case. How much
latitude political representatives ought to have has been hotly debated. This is known
as the mandate–independent controversy: Should MPs be delegates, merely conveying the opinion of the constituency, or should MPs be independent representatives,
deciding what is best for the constituency or the nation as a whole, regardless of the
opinions of their voters? The latter view is also, of course, the "burkian" approach,
often described as "virtual representation," meaning primarily that representatives
can act in the interests of people in whose name they act without even being elected
by them (see Pitkin 1967, 171–79).[1]

Today, the role of representatives is, according to Jacques Thomassen (1994,
241), to participate in national legislation and policy-making processes—on behalf
of their constituencies. Despite a recent deliberative turn in democratic theory (e.g.,
Dryzek 2000), it is still widely agreed that democratic representation presupposes
a significant degree of policy agreement between the "principal" and its "agent."
MPs are delegates for those whom they are elected to represent. In this perspective,
substantive representation is to *act* "in the interests of the represented, in a manner
responsive to them" (Pitkin 1967, 209). However, as indicated, substantive representation is not only about behavior, but also about correspondence in policy views,
as representativeness in opinions is by and large strongly correlated to actual interest
representation through activity. This connection, however, is not necessarily linked
to similarities in terms of social background: wealthy members of Congress or Parliament might act as advocates for the poor.

Clearly, "the politics of presence" and "principal–agent" conceptions of representation may conflict. If MPs are a small-scale version of the electorate in every relevant
social respect, but fail to do what the voters want, they are representative in the first
sense but not the second; the reverse is true if they do what the voters want but
without being socially representative of them. In this book, we consider representation of political preferences to have normative priority over social representativeness,
in line with the delegate, or principal–agent, conception. Nevertheless, we believe
that both aspects have merit and will explore both empirically, not least to see if
possible changes in descriptive representation are followed by changes in substantive
representation. But first: through which mechanisms can parties make descriptive
and policy representation work?

HOW DO PARTIES PROVIDE REPRESENTATION?

Parties may contribute to descriptive and policy representation in different ways.
First, parties may provide representation by presenting both candidates and policies
to the voters and by competing for their support at elections. Second, they may
represent by conveying the policy preferences of the voters through their organizations—their membership and party activists—to the MPs and ministers. However,

on both normative and descriptive grounds, which mechanism is most important and whether they are, in fact, both beneficial has been much discussed. The difference is crucial and leads, we will argue, to opposing expectations when it comes to the consequences of mass membership party decline in terms of parties' representative capacity. Before turning to the party literature, let us begin by looking at the debate according to representation studies.

At first, studies of representation as delegation ignored parties altogether, focusing on the relationship between the constituency voters and their representative, independent of parties (Dalton, Farrell, and McAllister 2011, 22). A seminal article by Warren Miller and Donald Stokes (1963) on representation in the United States incorporated the delegate perspective. The authors compared the views of the constituency voters with the roll-call vote of Congress representatives, assuming that competition for votes would impact the voting record. They found different results for different policy areas, ranging from substantial correlation between voters' opinions and their representatives' votes to hardly any correlation (Miller and Stokes 1963, 55).

Eventually, it became clear that the Miller–Stokes model was not fully applicable in all systems and was biased toward US politics (Thomassen 1994, 243–45). The US system is characterized by relatively weak party discipline, unlike most other Western democratic systems (cf. Converse and Pierce 1986). In parliamentary systems, approaching the party government model (Wright 1971), party discipline must be ensured to secure effective government, and not much variance in roll-call voting is left when party affiliation is taken into account. As a consequence, studies focusing on individual roll-call voting will not make much sense. Parties, more than individual politicians, tend to be the main political actors in such democracies.

A second phase of representative studies, particularly in parliamentary democracies, has therefore focused on the relationship between voters and their preferred parties (e.g., Holmberg 1974; Barnes 1976; Thomassen 1994). Scholars have acknowledged that the individual relationships between MPs and voters are less relevant due to parliamentary selection of governments, PR electoral systems, and the relative strength of political parties. In parliamentary polities, parties are the most important vehicle for aligning preferences between voters and representatives, and consequently, *the responsible party mandate model of representation* is suggested as a better fit with empirical realities (Rose 1974; Katz 1987). The assumption is that political parties present policy alternatives before elections, voters vote for the party closest to their own policy views, and the parties' control and discipline in office must be sufficient to follow up on and implement the policy program (cf. the "party government model" mentioned above). The electoral competition between parties advocating different policy packages is what brings about proximity between party voter and MP preferences.[2]

A similar tension can be found again in the party literature. Party organizations are seen as an indispensable corollary of electoral competition (e.g., Robertson 1976, 1), but whether they should organize ordinary voters and be internally democratic has been disputed. Based on the American experience and a liberal–economic model of democracy, it is maintained that the democratic merit and legitimacy of parties rest above all on the competition between parties' advocating comprehensive programs among the voters (e.g., Schattschneider 1942; Schumpeter 1942; Wright 1971). Parties coordinate and simplify elite politics, making coherent government possible and offering the voters a political choice (Cox and McCubbins 1993). The party organization as such has not been seen as instrumental in creating representative political decision makers—quite the contrary. Members may be loyal voters and helpful during electoral campaigns, but internally, democratic membership parties often lead to debates and compromises, resulting in less distinct political alternatives for voters than those found in elite-dominated parties (Ranney 1951, 491; Downs 1957, 25). Thus, party membership organizations might distort, rather than enhance, policy congruence between voters and politicians.

May's (1973) famous law of a "curvilinear" relationship between the political preferences of voters, party activists, and party leaders illustrates the argument: it is assumed that leaders will generally take the middle position between the more moderate voters and the more ideological party activists. The reason is that the incentives for actors to become involved and succeed in politics differ. Party leaders must respond to the median, moderate voters to win elections. The rank-and-file activists, however, enter politics to fight causes and tend to propose more radical and distinct policies. Activists are less constrained by voters' support. Thus, representative democracy is—in May's perspective—sustained by electoral party competition, not by party organizations. Responsiveness to citizens' preferences requires that party leaders be held accountable to voters, not to members (McKenzie 1982, 195).

Seen from this perspective, the decline of mass membership organizations represents no great threat to parties' representative capacity. It could even represent a potential improvement, given that it implied less active and less influential "unrepresentative" members. The party elite's stronger position could be used to adapt to the preferences of the voters. For the sake of efficient party competition, that is, adaptation to the electorate and media demands, less member-dense parties could select candidates who better match the party electorate.

The opposite view can be found both in the majoritarian concept of democracy, as noted earlier, and in the "realist" liberal approach to democracy. The latter questions the democratic potential of linkage between party competition and elite responsiveness, especially in two-party systems. The argument is, first, that party leaders are also driven by policy views and have ideological convictions that do not support a pure vote-maximizing electoral strategy (Miller 1983, 150). Second, it is argued that in most Western democracies, elections are contested on multiple dimensions, which might be difficult to include in a single ballot every two to five years. Staying representative requires mechanisms enabling party communication with voters between elections. Voter surveys and party processes to develop new programs before the next election are two such mechanisms, as are the communication networks provided by party membership organizations (Allern and Pedersen 2007). Third, it has proven difficult to develop and establish significant new parties in the public political arena. As Ware (1979) points out, the "market of parties" has few "sellers," allowing these few to control the policies and/or quantity of "supplied alternatives." Consequently, established parties can, at least in the short run, resist new socio-political conflicts without risking electoral defeat.

In sum, competitive party systems do not straightforwardly carry out the purported task of fair preference aggregation (Ware 1979, 38, 43), but mass membership and intra-party democracy can compensate for the imperfect structure of the party systems (cf. Ware 1979, 78). Political leaders are seen as accountable to members and to voters, not in opposition to them (Assarson 1993, 49). Having numerous and powerful members may add to the representative capacity of parties by actively holding the MPs accountable for the party program they were elected to implement. In other words, parties provide a channel for participation, influence, and representation that supplements and deepens electoral democracy (Lawson and Merkl 1988).

In this perspective, which came to predominate among European party scholars, the decline of parties as membership organizations is likely to weaken the representative capacity of parties in public office. More elitist, top-down parties would lead to less representative MPs than those based on parties with a large, more influential membership organization. This is also the main assumption of Katz and Mair (1995), as outlined in chapter 1. Cartel parties will attract a different kind of party activist, as they have fewer members and are less dependent on membership support. This also makes it more likely that the party organization will select candidates and policies that alienate party supporters. If the pool of potential party candidates changes the social and political profiles of candidates and, eventually, of elected MPs may change as well (see also Mair 2006).

That said, the consequences of mass party decline for parties' representative capacity are not a given. Fewer members and more state financing—weakened mass parties—might result in a decline of representation by parties, but it depends on the importance of party organizations for representation compared to electoral competition. We cannot use the size of parties' membership organizations per se as a proxy for parties' ability to represent, nor can we take it for granted that electoral competition alone provides democratic representation. The consequences of mass party decline for electoral representation is a question to be explored empirically, and we believe that both competitive and organizational mechanisms play a part in the final result.

TOWARD AN ANALYTICAL MAP OF PARTIES' REPRESENTATIVE CAPACITY

Figure 2.1 summarizes the discussion so far by distinguishing between the representative capacity generated through party system competition and the party organization. The figure presents a simplified model of parties' representative capacity with two of the main channels, or mechanisms, for keeping MPs in line with their voters:

first, the electoral channel where parties operate as competitive actors and second, the party organizational channel.

As noted in chapter 1, we concentrate on parties as organized groups of members, activists, and MPs, treating the formal structures of party organizations as one of the internal factors that might influence parties' ability to represent at the different levels. We assume that parties in public office, party MPs, have multiple "principals" whose preferences do not necessarily converge. These include the central party organization, their territorial constituency party, the party voters, and the party members. We will concentrate on the latter two groups to be represented: voters and members. Among members, we distinguish between ordinary members and national congress delegates ("party activists").

We also need to distinguish between comparisons between the voters, members, delegates, and MPs within a particular party, and comparisons between all voters, all party members, all delegates, and all MPs. The specific party approach addresses how well the different layers within a single party represent the other levels; the second examines how well the party system as a whole represents the electorate. The average of the representative capacities of individual parties may well be different from the representative capacity of the party system as a whole. Both party-specific and the system-level congruence must be mapped over time.

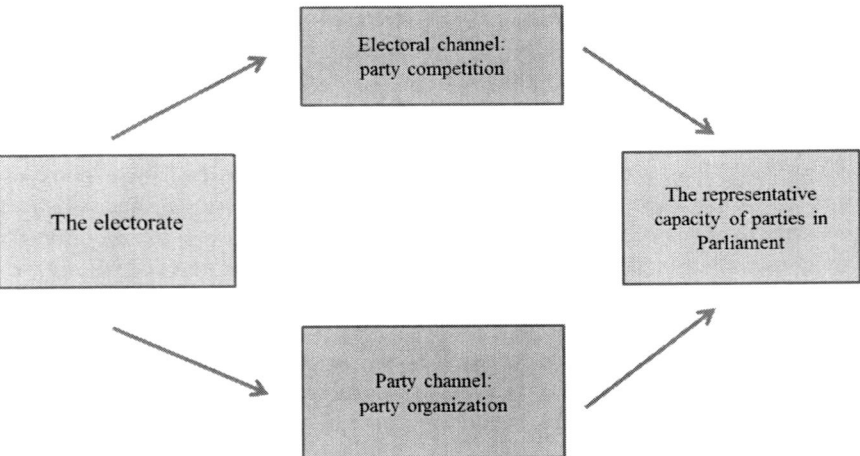

Figure 2.1. A simplified model of processes sustaining parties' representative capacity.

Next, we need to specify what party-based representation *through* membership organizations would imply. In debates on how parties make democracy work, we have seen that the representativeness of MPs could emerge from competition for votes. If electoral competition is efficient and dominates, it does not matter much if members and activists have become more different from voters: parties are in any case likely to balance lists of candidates to mirror the social composition and political profiles of the electorate at least to appear "in touch" with the electorate.[3] Yet, as implied by Alan Ware and others (e.g., Ware 1979), social and political representativeness can in theory be colored by those populating party organizations as well—to the extent that their backgrounds and policy views are channeled into parliamentary groups via candidate selection and the creation of party platforms. The representative capacity of the party organizations affects MPs' representativeness positively, provided that the profiles of party members and activists reflect the voters' interests, and negatively if party affiliates deviate from them. Conversely, if party members and delegates differ from the electorate, this might contribute to a weakened representative capacity in public office.

Thus, if the representativeness of party organizations has in fact declined, the ultimate representative capacity of parties in public office may also decline. The proposition in the decline of mass party debate, is that the pool of potential party candidates has changed as a consequence of a narrower membership base, thereby changing the social and political profiles of candidates, and finally, of the elected MPs as well. The parties may recruit less representative politicians. If so, it could be that there will be a continuous decline in representation capacity, or we might expect a "threshold effect," depending on the level of membership. And if there is a threshold, will it be triggered by falling below a certain number of members, or is it the percentage of voters that is crucial for a party's representative capacity? Such a threshold effect can only be discovered through empirical studies.

However, whether having fewer members means having "odder" members socially and ideologically is an empirical question in its own right. Such a development is not a given: the remaining members might—in theory—still represent voters satisfactorily. Finally, it should be noted that we also need to explore whether the parties' members or mid-level activists are in fact capable of influencing their parties. Having few and/or inactive members may make it more legitimate for the party leadership to disregard the policies developed within the organization. But if a decrease in membership figures in fact means weakened members' influence, a less representative membership and pool of potential candidates will probably not matter much. It is also possible that membership decline and increased opportunities for full-time party workers produces an activist core with career ambitions (van Biezen and Poguntke 2014), groups that think and act more like the office-seeking party leadership. If that is the case, May's law is not very relevant: even unrepresentative and influential party activists will choose candidates who appeal to the party voters.

MEASUREMENTS AND RESEARCH QUESTIONS

For the decline of mass membership parties to matter, parties' representative capacity in the public office has to depend on the capacity of *party organizations* to represent the voters. In this book, we will concentrate on the principal aspect of *representation*: congruence between the voters and the different layers within the party. We limit ourselves to *observed similarities/discrepancies* in terms of social characteristics and policy views between voters, members, party delegates, and elected representatives (MPs). The better the match in all parts of the chain, the higher the representative capacity achieved through the party organization.

Our general measure of representation capacity is thus twofold. First, we map the degree of *social congruence (social representation)* of voters at different levels within parties—from members to MPs. Second, we look at the substantive element, the political attitudes of the party layers, to see if there is *issue congruence* between the voters, members, delegates, and MPs (*policy representation*). If we find decreased congruence over time, this will indicate declining representative capacity. However, before embarking on this two-step analysis, we need to map membership activity, communication, and influence *within* parties. For party membership to facilitate representation, there must be *activity, communication,* and *processes of bottom-up influence* within the organization. We do not aim for a comprehensive study of internal party democracy, with all its intricacies (Cross and Katz 2013), but internal party life is a necessity if internal party representation is to work.

These three elements will be our indicators of *changes* in the parties' representative capacities. Full overall representative capacity would in theory mean an operative party democracy and a complete congruence between descriptive background characteristics and policy opinions at every level. In practice, this is clearly impossible. Still, high scores on all three indicators would indicate high representative capacity. The following are our primary research questions:

1. Have parties changed in recent decades in level of membership activity, degrees of cross-level communication, and bottom-up influence, and if so, have they generally declined as bottom-up channels of party representation?
2. Has the social representativeness of party organizations—party members and delegates—vis-à-vis voters changed, and if so, has it generally declined? Similarly, has the social representativeness of the party in parliament—the MPs—vis-à-vis voters changed over time, and if so, has it generally declined?
3. Has the political representativeness of party organizations—party members and delegates—vis-à-vis voters changed, and if so, has it generally declined? Similarly, has the political representativeness of the party in parliament—the MPs—vis-à-vis voters changed over time, and if so, has it generally declined?

As discussed extensively in these first two chapters, there are many reasons to expect a general decline of parties' representative capacity "after the mass party," even if these claims can be problematized on theoretical grounds. In the following, we address three specific empirical expectations based on the overall "decline thesis" (for which we have data to test in the Norwegian case):

First, based on the premise that declining membership numbers lead to *a marginalization of party members* in the decision-making process, we expect a decline in the level of member activity, communication between organizational levels, and in perceived bottom-up influence. We also expect that parties with no or slow decline in membership will have declined less in member activism, communication, and member influence than other parties. Moreover, we expect that the *types* of party activities will be of a less instrumental kind than before.

Second, the decline of mass parties is expected to lead to decreased *social congruence* between the different groups within the party organization and the voters in terms of social backgrounds. This is also a question for the parties' MPs. In measuring social congruence, class/occupation, education, age, and gender are central characteristics. In view of the weakened mass party arguments, we would also expect that parties with no or slower decline in membership will have declined less in terms of social congruence.

Third, we expect that the policy *preferences* (on key issues) of both party members and delegates will have become less congruent with the policy views of voters, and that issue congruence between party voters and party MPs will have also declined. We consider key issues to be related to the economic left–right axis, but also to newer cleavages/conflicts, like economic growth vs. environment protection and attitudes toward immigration. These issues are important to all parties, and they have been intensely debated in most electoral campaigns since the late 1980s. As such, they are central to the argument that parties have declined as representative channels.

Two methodological issues should be noted. One is related to the problem known as the "Ostrogorski paradox": a majority of voters may prefer one party's overall program over another party's platform, but there may still be only minority support for all of the different policy proposals included in its total package (Rae and Daudt 1976). In empirical studies of congruence between voters and their representatives—whether anchored in elitist or grassroots parties—this means that one cannot realistically expect a complete match between party representatives and their voters. Second, we know that internal agreement tends to be greater at the higher levels of the party hierarchy, whatever the social background of the MPs. On most issues, parties' MPs are more homogenous in their beliefs, echoing the party program. Whatever the case, we need to find out whether the social and political profiles of party members and activists do in fact increasingly differ from the composition of voters in "declining parties."

Finally, these expectations mainly concern old parties; they are less relevant for those parties established after the "golden age" of mass parties. In the debates on membership decline, this is not much discussed, but it is well known that the "new parties" that have been emerging since the 1960s and 1970s differed from the "old parties" from the start. They were generally less institutionalized and had another style of decision making. These parties could be populist and "top-down," like many of the right-wing anti-tax and anti-immigrant parties. They could also be "new politics" parties and formally super-democratic, like the emergent green parties (e.g., Deschouwer 2008). How this "newness" might affect their representative capacity is not discussed much in the decline of parties literature, and we will take a more "exploratory approach" to these types of parties.

OTHER FACTORS

The decline of party membership and increased public financing are clearly not the only changes that may affect how able parties are to represent. Parties' representative capacity hinges, of course, on several different external and internal factors. We note, just in passing, that there are additional channels for transmitting voter preferences to MPs than parties and elections, such as interest organizations, lobbying, action groups, and engaged individuals contacting their MPs. Institutional structures like presidential vs. parliamentary systems and electoral systems are clearly also central. Internally there are mechanisms to bring about more direct influence from members, for example, when parties elect leaders and select party candidates for public office. Some parties have introduced such measures precisely to compensate for declining membership figures (e.g., Scarrow and Gezgor 2010; Whiteley 2011; Scarrow 2015). Our central concern is with changes in the effects of the party organizational channel over time. Although we expect numerous changes to influence the development of parties' representative capacity, it is beyond the scope and potential of this study to identify the most significant drivers of stability and change.

However, we will still single out three factors for some more inspection, all worth keeping in mind in light of the discussion above. First, electoral competition is the alternative channel of representation in our analytical model. To what extent do parties need to chase voters, and how strongly do they compete with each other today, compared to the 1970s and 1980s? Second, the nomination process is both a potential arena for member influence and a product of the external electoral system, and a feature that may itself affect the extent to which party organizations are able to control MPs. Do parties still control candidate selection, or do voters have a say today? And finally, the formal organizational structure is defining the context of intra-party influence and a central feature of the old mass party model. What are the formal structures of party organization: have bottom-up communication and influence become more or less likely over time? Although this book does not aim at a full-blown study of the drivers of change in parties' representative capacity, these features touch directly upon the processes we describe, and we will return to them both in our description of the case of Norway and in our concluding chapter.

CONCLUSION

The purpose of this chapter has been, first, to define the concept of "representation" and to discuss the theoretical grounds for the (hypo)thesis predicting the decline of parties' representative capacity. The second main purpose has been to develop an "analytical map" that enables us to study the development empirically in a more systematic and comprehensive way, with a particular emphasis on the organizational channel. Full overall representative capacity is argued to consist of complete congruence in descriptive background characteristics and policy opinions at every level between party voters and party officials. Activity, communication, and influence among party members are seen as necessary conditions; otherwise, there is no reason to attribute any weight to the membership organization in terms of supplementing (or distorting) party congruence between voters and representatives.

NOTES

1. Burke, in his speech to the electors of Bristol (Nov. 3, 1774), argued that representatives should serve the constituency's interest but not necessarily its will.

2. See also the discussions in Matthews and Valen (1999) and Rohrschneider and White-field (2012, 2–7).

3. Parties do this as autonomous actors, of course, but they are stimulated by the competition for votes.

3

Parties' Representative Capacity

What Do We Know?

In this first part of our empirical inquiry we map and review studies that throw light on the development of parties' representative capacity over the last decades. What can research on voters, party members, and MPs tell us about relevant changes, within and across countries? This review cannot be a genuine meta-analysis due to lack of directly comparable designs and data, but it highlights that we do have some systematic knowledge to lean on. Informatively, we find that research on *changes* in parties' representative capacities is fairly limited. Few recent studies on the descriptive and substantive representativeness of MPs link their findings to, or include, an analysis of possible changes among party members, activists, or party finance.

We address the three specific research questions specified in chapter 2: first, the possible changes in the internal members' activities and influence; second, the social representativeness of different party levels; and third, their political representativeness. In a fourth part, we also highlight the (very few) studies targeting the balance between the electoral and organizational channels in providing input to party policies.

THE DEVELOPMENT OF MEMBERSHIP
ACTIVITY AND BOTTOM-UP INFLUENCE

Party organizations' capacity to provide representation, must build on the rank-and-file activities that are instrumental in channeling voter preferences upwards to the party elites. Have the decline of membership figures and increase in public finance led to less active and less influential party members?

There are few *membership activity* studies—comparative or over time—that are reported in the literature (see Heidar 2006). Research on levels and types of activity is mostly done at one point in time, confined to one nation, and often to single parties. The way activism is operationalized reflects the analytical focus of the particular research, making cross-country summaries difficult. However, let us try to sum up the main findings, starting with the scattered descriptions from the very beginning of our period.

Early membership surveys found that many joined their party primarily as a general expression of support, sometimes labelled as "credit card membership." After joining, they were fairly inactive, and had no intention of becoming an active member (Heidar 2006). A number of case studies also show that the individual level of activity was in the range "moderate to low" before the widespread membership decline accelerated throughout the 1980s and 1990s. In the German Christian Democratic Union (CDU) in the 1970s, roughly one-third of members attended at most one party function annually (Falke 1982, 73).

Later, in the 1990s, up to 50 percent of British Labour Party members, and 75 percent of Conservative Party members, were reported to be inactive during an average month (Whiteley and Seyd 2002, 95–97). Surveys of Norwegian party members (in 1991 and 2000) showed that more than 50 percent did not take part in any activities whatsoever during the preceding year. About 20 percent also stated they had no intention of being active within the party (Heidar and Saglie 2003a, 770). At the turn of the last century, only 7–8 percent of members in the Danish Liberal and Christian parties were classified as "active," which was defined as spending more than five hours monthly on party activities (Pedersen et al. 2004, 375). In Ireland, eight of ten Fine Gael members (in 1999) responded that they were "fairly active" when comparing themselves to an "average member." Over 50 percent spent no time at all on party activities in an average month (Gallagher and Marsh 2004, 413). This also indicates that norms and realities do not go hand in hand. A survey of members in five federal Canadian parties in 2000 found that two out of three had attended two party events or less the previous year, one in three none at all (Cross and Young 2004, 439).

When summarizing studies from before 2000, Scarrow ([2000] 2002, 95) stated that the proportion of members participating in party activities on a regular basis varied from 10 percent to 45 percent. Gauja estimated—based on party surveys and other sources from a number of countries—that only a fraction of party members (approximately 9 percent) were active before 2000 (Gauja 2013b, 128). A study of party activism based on voter survey data from 36 countries in 2004 (ISSP-data[1]) showed that less than 4 percent of the electorate were active within parties (Whiteley 2011, 24). Naturally, the most demanding and time consuming activities engage the smallest share of members. In other words, and in spite of diverging study design and operationalization, there are solid grounds for claiming that member activity early in the period, as discussed here, was fairly low. Whether the figures from the latter part of this period indicate stability or change since the 1980s, however, is difficult to say.

An early Swedish party study based on voter, and not membership surveys looked at changes over a longer period of time, basically pre-dating the period studied here. It covered all major parties and spanned a thirty-year period from 1960 to 1994

(Widfeldt 1999a, 137–40, 150). Although there were some changes in question regarding wordings and a "small numbers" problem, the data indicated a declining trend in party activity from the late 1970s until the early 1990s. Attending party meetings fluctuated in the period, but was, in the 1990s, down to 4.0 percent of the total electorate from a former level of 6.5 percent. On the other hand, membership numbers declined rather modestly in the period, from 11 percent to 10 percent from 1968 to 1994 according to these surveys.

Whiteley and Seyd (1998, 115) found that British parties were de-energized in terms of member activism between 1990 and 1994. Gauja reports, based on party surveys and other sources from a number of Western countries, that membership activity is "a pervasive problem both across democracies and party types" (Gauja 2013a, 95). However, both Heidar et al. (2012) in their study of Norwegian parties from the 1990s onwards and Spier et al. (2011) in their study of the two major German parties from 1998 to 2009, found a stable or even an increasing level of party member activity. They also found that the level of activity was not very high; it was fairly stable at a low level.

Research on the number of public positions to be filled by the parties at local levels suggests that there is at least a bottom-line for the active members needed by parties to uphold their position as public utilities in democratic systems (Sundberg 1987; van Biezen 2004b). We can, therefore, conclude on two notes. First, it seems well documented that many members today do not seek an active role within the party (van Biezen and Poguntke 2014, 209). Second, it is a moot point whether the activity of party members in general has *declined* accordingly across parties and countries.

On the second issue, the *internal patterns of influence* potentially linking members' and activists' opinions with party policies and the policy views of MPs, the "decline thesis" predicts a trend toward weakened internal democracy, partly driven by declining membership and activity, and partly by professionalization and increased finance. Moreover, external forces may be driving this change, like the mediatization of politics and the personalization of political communication (e.g., Katz 2013). The empirical study on internal party democracy is clearly challenging. Cross and Katz (2013) argue that just like in the study of democracy in general, the topic of party democracy is slippery. Is internal party democracy primarily about participation, inclusiveness, centralization, accountability, or something else altogether (Cross and Katz 2013, 3)? There are no definitive answers to the normative and empirical questions raised in these debates. Keeping that in mind, and concentrating on the actual involvement and influence of members and activists, what do empirical studies suggest about change as parties decline?

In her comparative study of parties in the UK, Australia, and New Zealand, Gauja (2013a) looks at the structures and processes that shape party policies or, more precisely, the mechanisms linking the members' political preferences to the political outcome found in the parliamentary party groups. The analysis spans the years between 1997 and 2012, and "concentrates on the process that enables policy preferences to be articulated" (Gauja 2013a, 3). Gauja found that parties *still* channel members' preferences and that small-sized parties provide better opportunities for formal participation in decision-making processes. Another finding was that these opportunities were dominated by a small core of members, but with the acquiescence of the general membership (218). However, the members' input was only a part of the processes influencing parliamentary party policies. Although the party members clearly had their advocates inside the parliamentary groups, parliamentary politics was, to some extent, disconnected from the party organization. Members of Parliament had several masters and sought, in their role perception, to balance the demands of the party, the parliament, and the constituency.

Few studies include longitudinal data that could help in our search for changes in members' power. The renewed interest found within many parties for broader nomination processes, like primaries, indicates that party elites would like to reduce the power of party activist (see, e.g., Hazan and Rahat 2010; Rahat, Hazan, and Katz 2008). However, there are also dissenting voices to the decline perspective. In his study of the Swedish parties in 1960–1994, before and early in our period, Widfeldt concluded that the members' potential influence, as reflected in party organizational statutes, was as least as great in the 1990s as in the 1960s (Widfeldt 1999a, 231). In a more recent study of decision-making in the Swedish social democratic party in 1950 compared to 1990, the argument is made that the leadership had actually *less* control over policy debates and activists in 1990s than in the 1950s, which indicate more rather than less democracy (Loxbo 2013). We may add that the general assumption in the party literature is that the organizational control of communication and members' lives has decreased. This literature also states that at the same time, media politics have forced the party leadership to be more hands-on, given less time to democratic internal party processes. Less control over the activists does not necessarily indicate that party elites have less power in their parliamentary parties. Still, Loxbo (2013, 550) has a point in warning against idealizing the democratic qualities in the mass parties of the past. A fairly standard summary of available literature states that political parties today appear "powerful and rich but devoid of internal energy and at odds with the external environment"(Ignazi 2014, 166).[2]

Empirical studies show that there is a low level of party member activity. However, it is not clear whether the activities of the average member have declined or not. Possibly, there has always been one small group of members that are fairly active, and another much larger group that do not bother to even think about being more active. Scholars by and large believe that activism among the party membership has declined, but there is not enough hard evidence to bring out the changes over time. Some evidence even points to stability and rise. An important distinction, which we shall return to later, is between decline in activism *among* the registered party members and decline of overall activism *within* parties. One possibility is that as membership numbers decline, the levels of activity among the *remaining* members stayed constant, or even increased. Combine this with the decreasing membership numbers, and *overall activism in parties* might have declined, even if the *active share of the present membership* has remained constant or has increased.

The current level of member activity is reported low in almost every study. It is, therefore, highly likely that the overall member activity within parties has declined. Another matter is that even if the overall level of party activism has declined, there may still be *sufficient* activity within the parties to uphold the representative capacity of the party organizations.

THE DEVELOPMENT OF SOCIAL REPRESENTATION

The next question is whether parties have become less socially representative for voters since the 1970s and 1980s. First, it is important to note that there has always been a gap between voters, members, and party representatives in public office in terms of descriptive characteristics. Robert Putnam coined many years ago the law of increasing disproportion, which stated that "the higher the level of political authority, the greater the representation of high-status social groups" (Putnam 1976, 33). We also know that party members "have never been an accurate mirror of the population" (Scarrow and Gezgor 2010, 828). Survey research from around 1990 in 15 West-European countries by and large found male domination, older than average members, higher educational levels among members than among voters, and an under-representation of working-class citizens (Widfeldt 1995).

In a study based on survey data from 36 countries in 2004, it was found (again) that members were older, more likely male, and of higher social status than voters (Whiteley 2009, 135). Like other forms of high intensity participation, party members tended to be above average in terms of income, age, and education across a wide range of countries and types of parties.[3] There is a difference, however, between the conventional forms of participation, like party membership, and the non-institutionalized forms, like signing petitions and demonstrating. Non-institutionalized participation had a stronger presence of women and the youth, although in this arena, we note increases in inequalities based on education (Marien, Hooghe, and Quintelier 2013, 205). Studies of the demographic and social discrepancies between voters and MPs also show clear gaps in social and demographic descriptive characteristics. Parliamentarians are on average more often male, older, better educated, and with higher social status than voters (Putnam 1976; Best and Cotta 2000; Gallagher, Laver, and Mair 2011).

Have these discrepancies decreased and remained stable, or have they increased during our period as suggested by the party decline thesis? An increased social distance between voters and members would give the parties less representative capacity. In his book on Swedish party members and activists (1960–1994), Widfeldt found little evidence of decreasing descriptive representativeness apart from the age variable (Widfeldt 1999a). Moreover, there were signs of increased gender representativity. Recently, Scarrow and Gezgor (2010) presented a longitudinal study to analyze the consequences of reduced party memberships since 1989. This was based on European Social Survey and Eurobarometer data. They found a mixed picture of changes in descriptive representativeness and concluded that party membership decline had "not meant that parties' grassroots had become some kind of odd subculture, no longer able to provide legitimacy because they were too different from the rest of society" (Scarrow and Gezgor 2010, 839). It emerged that the party members had become older relative to voters, but on variables like income, union membership, and religiosity, they were actually more like the voters in the 2000s than in the 1990s.[4]

Some research points to generational change as a source of declining representativeness, and also that the low recruitment of young party members is part of a trend in political participation away from its traditional forms (Young 2013, 77–78). Another recent change is the relative increase of female party members also noted by Widfeldt. This was found in seven out of 12 West European countries between the 1990s and the 2000s (Childs 2013, 85). This finding is strengthened by research showing that the share of women within party hierarchies and among party candidates has increased substantially over the last decades, even though gender parity is rare (Kittilson 2013, 3).

What about the *social representativeness of the MPs?* In studies of recruitment in national assemblies, there has been a tendency toward declining descriptive representativeness, notably on gender, age, education, and social background. The profile of MPs from the 1980s onwards has turned more elitist and professional. Analyses of comprehensive data for parliaments over the last 150 years in Western Europe, supplemented with data from Eastern Europe from 1990, show some clear trends in the social background of MPs in the years up to 2006 (Best 2007; Best and Cotta 2000). The largest change is found in the increased presence of women in parliaments, more than doubling their share to just below 30 percent. This makes the underrepresentation of women somewhat less dramatic than it used to be (Best 2007, 96–103). The mean age of MPs' entry into parliaments has remained fairly stable at around 45, making parliamentarians in general older than the general population. However, this is not a rising trend. The rise in educational level started around 1945 and continued after 1980. The share with a university education in 2006 was close to 70 percent. The presence of lawyers has declined steadily during the whole twentieth century, although they still make up 6 to 7 percent in the 2000s, making this group grossly overrepresented. The blue collar workers' group has continued to decline, while the public sector employees levelled off around 1990, but stabilized within the 40 and 50 percent range. There has also been a rise in the share of party and pressure group officials, which make a case for growing professionalization of European parliamentarians. In Best's view, the longitudinal data on the MPs show the emergence of a representative elite and a process of political professionalization (Best 2007, 110–11).

Summing up these studies, we must again note that longitudinal and comparative studies of party members and activists are few. Published research still indicates rather clearly that party members—although still a high-status group compared to voters—are increasingly becoming more similar to the voters, particularly when looking at the presence of women. The exception is the rather stable discrepancy of age. As for MPs, studies indicate that they are increasingly becoming less similar to the general population, and that this gap has been widening in the years since the 1980s. The exception again is that the underrepresentation of women has become less prominent. Empirical studies do not confirm the expectations of less socially representative party members and MPs after the mass party.

THE DEVELOPMENT OF POLICY REPRESENTATION

Have party members and activists become more out of tune with the political preferences of party voters over the last decades? Has the same happened with the MPs, as compared to their voters? Starting with the *party members,* the studies by Widfeldt—although they were based on data largely predating the relevant period—can serve as a reference point (Widfeldt 1999a; 1999b). Widfeldt's research was partly based on longitudinal Swedish data, and partly on cross-sectional data from voter surveys from several European national election studies around 1990 (Widfeldt 1995). The Swedish data show average self-placement on the left-right scale comparing MPs, party activists, party members, and voters from 1985 to 1994. As expected, the members placed themselves in somewhat more extreme positions than the party voters: left party members placed themselves more to the left, and right party members placed themselves more to the right—not much, but measurable. This voter-member gap increased over the years, giving reason to conclude that there was a decline in the representative capacity of Swedish party members during the period (Widfeldt 1999b, 325). In the comparative study on 37 parties in 15 countries, the findings on voter-member self-placements (again, along the left-right scale) was the same as in the Swedish case: there was a tendency, although fairly small, for party members to be more extreme than party voters (1995, 167).

These findings have been corroborated by numerous studies. Although there is a difference between party voters and party members, the difference is generally small.[5] More recent case studies have shown either very few disparities of any sort between members and voters (Gallagher and Marsh 2002, 170), or a tendency toward increasing polarization at higher levels of the party hierarchy (Buch Jensen 1999, 143; Holmberg 2000, 168; Norris 1995; Narud and Skare 1999; Bäck and Möller 1997, 118). Some studies also report that the grass-root activists are by and large more moderate than higher level activists (Young 2013, 79). However, we know less about how politically representative party activists and party organization elites are (compared to the voters)—not to mention whether and how this has changed over the last decades.

Scarrow and Gezgor (2010) did, like Widfeldt (1995), do a comparative analysis on European parties, but added a time dimension. They based their study on Eurobarometer and European Social Surveys (ESS) from the 1990s and the 2000s, which are within the period when we expect change to happen. Looking at the mean left-right self-placement, they, however, found a striking stability in the members' policy representation of voters. Although members were (again) slightly more ideologically extreme than the party supporters, this pattern did not change over the two decades. Only in three of thirteen parties did the data show a statistically significant difference, and the changes were just as much toward the comparative moderation of party members, as toward their radicalization (Scarrow and Gezgor 2010, 836). They found no trend indicating that declining membership had left parties to enroll only the most radical of their supporters or that the drops have made party systems more polarized (836). They concluded that Duverger's mass party, a term that for him also meant "the party of the masses," had turned into "the party of the mean" during the period with declining membership figures (840).[6] Spies and Kaiser (2014, 576–90) suggest that representativeness on the left-right policy dimension today depends on the degree of grass root involvement: parties in which the elites decide on the nomination of candidates, (paradoxically) show a slightly higher level of representative congruence than parties with more inclusive selectorates.[7] Hence, the stability over time in political representativeness, as demonstrated by Scarrow and Gezgor (2010), might in some cases have been affected by organizational reforms. We must bear in mind, however, that these analyses rely on self-placement along the left-right axis, and not on policy views on particular issues.

The huge number of studies on *policy congruence between voters and MPs* do not reveal evidence of a notable decline in congruence in spite of the widening *social* gap between these groups. As mentioned in chapter 2, in their groundbreaking study, Miller and Stokes (1963) found substantial congruence between US voters' opinion and the roll call voting behavior of their representatives on the issues of social welfare and civil rights. On the other hand, there was hardly any correlation for foreign policy issues. The body of research following Miller and Stokes' footsteps, including studies on European parliamentary democracies based on the party mandate model, finds fairly strong and fairly stable policy congruence.[8]

Thomassen (2012) criticizes parts of this literature for providing an excessively optimistic view of political representation. His argument is that most of these studies—the comparative studies in particular—rely too much on measuring the left-right dimension, rather than looking at specific issues. Studies suggest that congruence is worse on specific issues (Belchior 2012; Thomassen 2012; Costello, Thomassen, and Rosema 2012). Moreover, Holmberg (2011, 58–62), when analyzing a number of specific issues, observed a small decline in congruence in Sweden from 1968 to 2006, but the decline was not evident in all parties. In the Netherlands, on the other hand, congruence between voters and MPs essentially increased after the 1970s. The trend is best described as fluctuating over time, both for the left-right dimension and specific issues (e.g., Andeweg 2011, 50–51).

Widfeldt (1999b, 317) found no evidence of a decline in the political representativeness of parliamentarians compared to their voters between 1985 and 1994. The MPs, however, were not representative of their voters from the outset, as the MPs placed themselves in a somewhat more extreme position on the left-right scale. Nonetheless, the difference was not inordinate and, more importantly, the lack of congruence did not increase. Based on the analysis on the voter-parliamentarian policy divide, Widfeldt concluded in 1999 that there was no representative crisis in Sweden (324–25). However, in Ireland in the late 1990s, Gallagher and Marsh found a bigger difference between MPs and party voters than between voters and members in the Fine Gael party (2002, 169).

To sum up, neither the party members and activists nor the parties' MPs seem to be fully representative of the party voters in terms of policy positions. The prime instrument to measure this—self-placement along the left-right scale—is, however, somewhat problematic. Most likely, it will be interpreted differently at different levels of political participation and engagement. On the other hand, it is argued that the left-right dimension is the most powerful policy indicator when it comes to organizing individuals' political thought and behavior, particularly as single policy issues may not generally be so present in the mind of the voters (Belchior and Freire 2013, 285). Whatever the validity of the left-right scale in this type of research, there are few indications that the policy congruence of voters, members, activists, and MPs have changed or declined systematically throughout Western Europe after party membership plummeted and public finance of parties increased.

ELECTORAL COMPETITION VS. ORGANIZED LINKAGE

A few studies have also discussed the relative importance of electoral competition and organizational processes for impacting parties' policy positions in parliaments. These studies mainly use surveys, but also refer to experts' opinions and manifesto data. Based on the Comparative Study of Electoral Systems and other recent cross-national data, Dalton, Farrell, and McAllister (2011) question the generally negative diagnosis of a declining party-based democracy. They study five forms of contemporary party linkage, which include election campaigns, participation, ideology, representation, and policies (16–17). They find that political parties still dominate the electoral process in shaping the discourse of campaigns, selection of candidates, and mobilizing citizens to vote. The voters for their part (not surprisingly) do not support parties that match their own political preferences. In addition, parties deliver the policies demanded by their voters, provided they win positions of power. Parties connect citizen preferences to the choice of representatives, with strong congruence between voters' and their party's left-right positions. Voter preferences are later translated into policies through the formation of (coalition) governments. Even if there is a decline in the organizational grass root linkage of parties, this does not affect their ability to represent, since they adapt through electoral competition (215–18). However, the study is not based on longitudinal (survey) data and cannot tell us if there have been changes in the alternative linkage mechanisms over time. Moreover, it does not discuss the issue of whether the party organization supplements electoral competition, and whether organizational processes sustain the parties in advancing new policies.

Rohrschneider and Whitefield (2012), on the other hand, ask whether party competition for votes is the only mechanism supporting policy congruence between voters and party representatives, or if the party organization, the complementary opinion-party linkage, still contributes to the representative capacity of parties (Rohrschneider and Whitefield 2012, 4). Their research is based on several expert surveys on parties in both Western and Eastern Europe from the 2003–2008 period, Manifesto data, and European Social Survey data (2003 and 2007). The policy indicator is (again) self-placements along the left-right scale. Their main finding is that the mass party is still a critical factor in providing voter-party congruence (180). This is not due to high membership figures, but in Western Europe, there are still parties (with a hierarchical structure and links to civil society) that contribute to limited policy distance between the voters and their parties, in contrast to the hollow shells dominating in Eastern Europe. Strong party organizations help keep party policies in line with their voters to a greater extent than the more shaky and unstable party organizations of the East (176). This study is also based on data from one point in time and do not deal with changes in membership figures and party finance.

From a somewhat different perspective, Ezrow et al. (2011) asked whether parties responded to the changing preferences of their supporters (i.e., the voters intending to vote for the party) or to the electorate at large (all voters). The study was based on the analysis of the left-right positions of parties and their voters over the period 1973 to 2003 in 15 Western European countries. The data were taken from the Manifesto Project and Eurobarometer surveys. They divided the parties into two groups: the mainstream parties (belonging to the Social Democratic, Conservative, Christian Democratic, and the Liberal party families) and the niche parties (Communist, Nationalist, and Green party families). Two main findings emerged from this study. First, changes in the mean voter position cause a corresponding shift in the mainstream parties' policy position (Ezrow et al. 2011, 288). Hence, parties seem to adapt to changes in voter opinion. Second, the niche parties were unresponsive to changes in the mean voter position. The reason was that ideologically oriented parties are responsive to the shifts in their supporters' position (288). In other words, the mainstream parties fight for the general vote just as a Downsian perspective would predict, while the niche parties operate in the electoral arena to spread their party-defined creed and attract a specific voter segment. This is a conclusion in support of the argument that party organizational processes count more in the niche parties.

Another study by Belchior and Freire (2013), which also differentiates between the different types of parties, makes a similar point. Empirically, Belchior and Freire base their study from 2008 on surveys on voters and MPs in Portugal. To measure policy preferences, they use both self-placements on the left-right scale and summary indices of 19 substantive policy issues covering left-right issues, as well as the libertarian-authoritarian dimension (new vs. old politics). Differentiating between the catch-all parties and the ideological ones, they find that on the whole, there is a better policy congruence for the so-called catch-all parties than for the ideological parties. The first are presumably more sensitive to the electoral changes. They also note that the differences are not huge (Belchior and Freire 2013, 285).

In short, existing studies on the impact of electoral competition versus party organization for creating voter-MP policy congruence *do not* suggest a declining overall party congruence. However, these studies do not clarify our main question. The persistent ability to create congruence is either mainly due to the fact that party members and the party organizations have not changed much or that party competition for votes makes parties respond. Another alternative of course is that both mechanisms might be at play.

CONCLUSION

A premise in the decline of parties' literature is that the demise of the mass party and the rise of catch-all and cartel parties came at the expense of a decline in party democracy. More precisely, declining membership and activity, along with increased public finance, cleared the way for a weakened representative capacity of parties, both socially and politically. Has empirical research substantiated these claims? In the studies surveyed, there are shades of the certain, the probable, and the unknown. Let us summarize what we consider the best claims for what happened to the mass parties and their representative capacity over the three decades since the 1980s.

First, there is probably a declining overall member activity within the electorate as a whole, but there is no indication that the members remaining in the parties are less active. Parties are perhaps less internally democratic than they used to be, although there is no reason to idealize democracy in the mass parties of the past. *Second*, in terms of social representation there is no trend for party members to be less representative of party voters. The parties' MPs, on the other hand, have continued the post WWII trend to become more exclusive, widening the gap with their voters, although with one exception: gender. *Third*, there is no trace of a widening gap in policy representation either for party members or for the MPs during this period.

That said, studies on the descriptive and substantive representativeness of MPs rarely link their findings to, or include, possible changes among party members and activists. The claim that party organizations as agencies of representation have declined has, in our view, neither been confirmed nor rejected by existing research. As noted earlier, one reason for this is the limited and not very reliable data on party members and activists. Another reason is that longitudinal data are close to non-existing, or rather impressionistic. This makes it difficult to evaluate the long-term effects of the changing activity levels within party organizations. The effects of a declining membership and changing party organizations on the policies of parties within democratic institutions are simply not addressed in the empirical analyses. The access to such data material in the Norwegian case is, therefore, highly relevant for the study of the decline of mass parties and their representative capacity in general.

NOTES

1. The International Social Survey Programme (ISSP) Citizenship Study of 2004, see http://www.issp.org.

2. Based on data from 36 countries in the 2004 International Social Survey Programme (ISSP) it has been shown that party members were very active in contacting the media, supporting demonstrations, signing petitions, and attending political meetings (Whiteley 2009, 140). But these are reports from activities external to the party organizations.

3. See for example Verba, Nie, and Kim 1978; Whiteley, Seyd, and Richardson 1994; Widfeldt 1995; Whiteley and Seyd 2002; Gallagher and Marsh 2004; Heidar and Saglie 2002; van Haute and Gauja, 2015.

4. These studies were based on national surveys. Consequently, the figures on party members have considerable uncertainty. As long as party members typically constitute 3 to 6 percent of the electorates, the total N for party members was rather small. Average N for the countries included in Scarrow and Gezgor (2010) is 58 in the 2000s. The countries are not explicitly stated in the article but the reference to Widfeldt's (1995) study makes it probable that they also study the same 15 Western European countries as Widfeldt (1995).

5. See summary and references in Scarrow and Gezgor 2010, 835–36. See also Young 2013, 79.

6. Ezrow et al. 2011 also argues that parties adapt to the mean voter.

7. See also the work of Hazan and Rahat 2010.

8. For the relevant literature, see, e.g., Miller and Stokes 1963; Holmberg 1974, 2000; Barnes 1976; Converse and Pierce 1987; Thomassen 1994; Esaiasson and Holmberg 1996; Matthews and Valen 1999; Dalton 1985; Schmitt and Thomassen 1999; Miller et al. 1999.

4

Norwegian Parties

Prospects for Representation

Norway is a small, stable, rather consensual democracy characterized by a unitary structure, parliamentary government, a proportional representation election system, multi-party politics, and coalition governments (Lijphart 2013). The country is ranked as one of the strongest democracies in the world, and is characterized as a high trust society in the comparative literature (Norris 2011; Delhey and Newton 2005).[1] Parties still dominate electoral campaigns, control elected institutions at all levels, and enjoy fairly strong (although declining) identification among the electorate (see, e.g., Bergman and Strøm 2011). Like in other European democracies, the media arena has become more central. Recently, social media have started to influence political debates and electoral campaigns in Norway, but not to an extent where the role of party organizations is undermined. At the same time, as mentioned in chapter 1, Norwegian parties have been challenged by numerous societal and institutional changes since the 1970s. Most importantly, they have experienced a steep decline in membership numbers, and public finance of parties has increased considerably over the last 20 years. Consequently, Norway is well-suited for researching the alleged changes in the representative capacity of party organizations in-depth.

In this chapter, we will first present the Norwegian parties: who are they and what have been the major political issue conflicts between them in the last decades? The discussion includes a brief evaluation of how the pattern of competition for votes has developed in recent decades to provide context to our empirical analysis on policy congruence in chapter 7, and to throw light on how well the electoral channel works in Norway. Second, we will document the extent to which the parties in question have changed in terms of membership decline and rise in public party finance in more detail. How strongly have Norwegian parties, as organizations, been stimulated to move away from voters? Thereafter, we will move on to map stability and change in other external and party-internal factors that may directly influence the development of parties' representative capacity in all its guises. More precisely, we will focus on candidate selection and the organizational structures of parties. Finally, in this chapter, we will present the data used in the subsequent empirical analyses.

THE PARTIES AND PARTY COMPETITION

The Norwegian parties and party system date back to the struggle between the conservatives and the liberals over constitutional reform and parliamentary democracy in the 1880s.[2] According to Stein Rokkan's model for socio-political cleavages, the first party establishments reflected both a territorial center/periphery cleavage and a socio-cultural conflict. The latter reflected linguistic differences, conflicts between the elites of the capital and the national bureaucracy, and a political alliance between a rural, populist-nationalist movement protecting traditional values, and a radical urban opposition to the political hegemony of the civil service. Later, other cross-cutting cleavages appeared. The main division emerged within the labor market: a left and right axis dividing the socialist and non-socialist parties (Rokkan 1967, 372ff.; Valen and Rokkan 1974; Heidar 2001). Between the 1930s and the early 1970s, Norway had one of the most stable party systems in Western Europe consisting of a conservative party (*Høyre*), a social-liberal party (*Venstre*), a social democratic party (*Arbeiderpartiet*), an agrarian party (*Bondepartiet*, later *Senterpartiet*), and a Christian party rooted in the Lutheran laymen's movement (*Kristelig Folkeparti*).

The Norwegian parties and the competition between them still reflect these old cleavages, but recent political changes have resulted in a more open and fluid party system (Heidar 2005; Knutsen 2004; Aardal 2011). In this book, we cover the seven parties with more or less consistent parliamentary representation since the 1970s until today, namely, from the left to the right of the political spectrum, the Socialist Left (SV), the Labour Party (Ap), the Centre Party (Sp),[3] the Christian People's Party (KrF), the Liberals (V), the Conservatives (H), and the Progress Party (FrP).[4] Only the Socialist Left (a splinter group from the social democrats that became Norway's New Left) and the Progress Party (a populist new right party) were formed after 1960. The others are the same parties as those dominating between the 1930s and 1970s. The Liberals split over the EU-membership issue in 1972, and basically had to re-establish themselves as a party during the 1990s. They were reunited with the split off, pro-EU party in 1988. Three other parties—a left-wing, a regional, and a green party—have also enjoyed representation in recent decades, but only for short periods of time.[5]

What are the prospects for a decline of representation provided by the competition between these parties? The relatively modest level of party fragmentation in Norway, with only two new persistent parliamentary parties since the 1960s, could hint at a limited responsiveness toward the electorate's policy views. A broad consensus has developed among old parties on major economic and social issues, and no doubt this limits the range of what is regarded as feasible public policies by political elites, also in Norway. Studies of post-1945 change in party programs based on data from the Manifesto Project (Volkens and Klingemann 2002) show that the parties converged along the left-right axis during the 1970s and in the 1990s (Narud and Valen 2007b, 140ff.). Still, there appears to be no strong and persistent trend toward policy convergence among the parties. As we shall elaborate on below, they still reflect conflicting clusters of voter preferences in major political issues and enjoy ownership in different types of issues.

Table 4.1. Parties and parliamentary elections 1989–2013

	1989	1993	1997	2001	2005	2009	2013
Socialist Left Party (SV)	10.1	7.9	6.0	12.5	8.8	6.2	4.1
Labour Party (Ap)	34.3	36.9	35.0	24.3	32.7	35.4	30.8
Centre Party (Sp)	6.5	16.7	7.9	5.6	6.5	6.2	5.5
Christian Democratic Party (KrF)	8.5	7.9	13.7	12.4	6.8	5.5	5.6
Liberal Party (V)	3.2	3.6	4.5	3.9	5.9	3.9	5.2
Conservative Party (H)	22.2	17.0	14.3	21.2	14.1	17.2	26.8
Progress Party (FrP)	13.0	6.3	15.3	14.6	22.1	22.9	16.3
Others	1.8	2.7	1.8	4.5	2.0	1.4	4.6

Source: http://www.aardal.info/.

In the period we cover, the Socialist Left Party typically obtained between 5 and 10 percent of the vote.[6] The party attracts voters with a preference for redistributive and environmental friendly policies, and has established ownership on these issues. The Labour Party consistently attracted more than 30 percent of the electorate, and these voters are on average positive to redistribution and located toward the left and center-left of the dominant left-right dimension. The party has ownership on several issues, but is considered particularly well able by voters to handle care for elderly, health, and employment policies.

The size of the three centrist parties varies between 4 and 10 percent of the vote, although the Liberals consistently do worse than the other two, and have failed to reach the 4 percent threshold for adjustment seats several times in the period we cover. The Centre Party has, to a little extent, managed to expand issue ownership beyond issues directly linked to their position in the conflict structure. Hence, voters are mostly confident in the party's ability to handle local and regional policies. The Centre Party, however, has a very strong position on the opposition toward EU and EU membership. This ownership is reflected in the strong result in the 1993 national election, one year before the last EU referendum in Norway. The Christian Democrats still attract voters with religious (Christian) beliefs, and has established ownership on issues related to child and family policies, as well as issues related to combating poverty. Although voters might vote for the Liberal Party for a number of reasons, it is only the environmental issue that stands out as an issue that a substantial proportion of voters consider the party best able to handle.

The Conservative Party has been the dominant party on the right, but its popularity at the polls has fluctuated between 14 and 27 percent in the last decades. It has not always been the second largest party in parliament. The party attracts voters who are relatively well-off and positive toward private enterprise, and a reduced level of taxation. The Conservatives have established issue ownership on tax policies and have also enjoyed a high degree of confidence on educational policies. The Progress Party slowly increased its share of the vote to 22–23 percent in the 2005 and 2009 elections. They saw their support drop to 16 percent during the 2013 election (Aardal 2011). This decrease is related to the terrorist attacks by Breivik in Oslo and Utøya in July 2011 (Allern and Karlsen 2014b). Since the late 1980s, the party has emphasized and profited on the immigration issue, and has gained a considerable ownership on this area. In addition, the party has focused on reduced taxes and care for the elderly.

All in all, to some extent, parties in Norway emphasize and prioritize different issues. They also present voters with different policy alternatives. Voting records on economic issues have revealed significant policy distances in parliament. In fact, the frequency of disagreement among the parties regarding issues debated in the Storting has grown considerably since the mid-1970s (Rommetvedt 1991, 2005). In recent years, we have also experienced a certain degree of polarization of party competition for government. Following the end of the Labour Party's predominant position in the 1960s, the Norwegian party system comprised—in terms of government alternatives—two blocs divided along the left-right axis. Between 1961 and 2005, government alternated between single-party Labour minority governments and center-right or centrist (mostly minority) coalitions.[7] In 2005, a majority center-left coalition consisting of the Labour, Socialist Left, and the Centre Party governed for the first time together. From 2013, a coalition of two rightist parties has held office. This included the Progress Party for the first time, with formalized external supports of two centrist parties (Liberals and Christian People's Party). Since 2005, elections have presented voters with fairly clear government alternatives in ideological terms (Allern 2010c; Allern and Karlsen 2014b). Voters' perceptions of clear policy differences between parties also increased (Narud 2011, 202).

Turnout in Norwegian national elections dropped a few percentage points in the late 1980s, but on average, more than three-fourths (about 77 percent) of the Norwegian electorate participate in parliamentary elections. That is a sizeable turnout level, approaching the mean score of Western European countries during the early 2000s. Although turnout is more or less stable, there are signs of instability in the electorate. Electoral volatility has increased considerably since the 1960s (Aardal 2011). Aggregate volatility, in terms of the Pedersen index,[8] increased from about 4 percent in the 1950s to about 15 percent in the late 1980s, and was rather stable until it dropped to 6.8 percent in 2009. Individual volatility, the proportion of voters that change party preference from one election to the next, has also increased considerably (figure 4.1). Moreover, since 1965, the proportion of voters that decided what party to vote for during the campaign has soared.

This instability in the electorate is the result of general weakened links between voters and parties, but voters are far from choosing randomly between parties. The

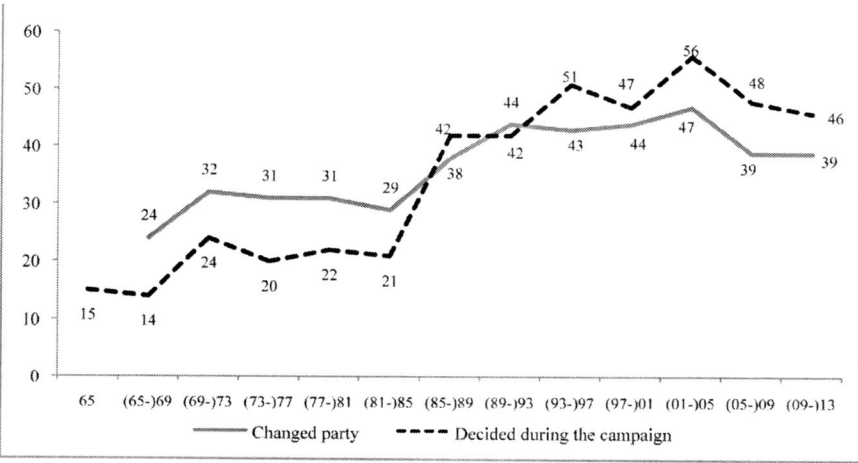

Figure 4.1. Instability in the Norwegian electorate: proportion of voters that changed party and decided what party to vote for during the campaign, 1965–2013. *Source: The Norwegian Election Study.*

relationship between ideology or political values and vote choice is strong (Karlsen and Aardal 2014). In a multiparty and multidimensional system like the Norwegian political system, stable political values do not unequivocally point in the direction of only one party. Rather, political predispositions define an area of acceptance that defines which parties the voters really consider voting for (Karlsen and Aardal 2014). As identification with one particular party is not strong, voters can more easily change between two or three parties.

On the whole, it seems as if parties do not compete as efficiently for the voter support as they used to, but that they increasingly have to chase voters and still offer them real alternative policy packages.

DECLINE IN PARTY MEMBERS

All parties in Norway operate with a clear, exclusive definition of a party member in their statutes (Heidar 2014). In terms of decision-making or organizational practices, one is either a member and an insider, or a member and an outsider. The members are operationally defined by registered membership and the payment of membership fees.[9] After the Labour Party phased out collective membership for the trade unions in the early 1990s, all parties have individual members only. Figure 4.2 shows the changes in total party membership from 1950 to 1990 in a five-year interval, and then yearly from 1990 to 2012. Before summarizing the main trends, a brief methodological note of caution is needed.

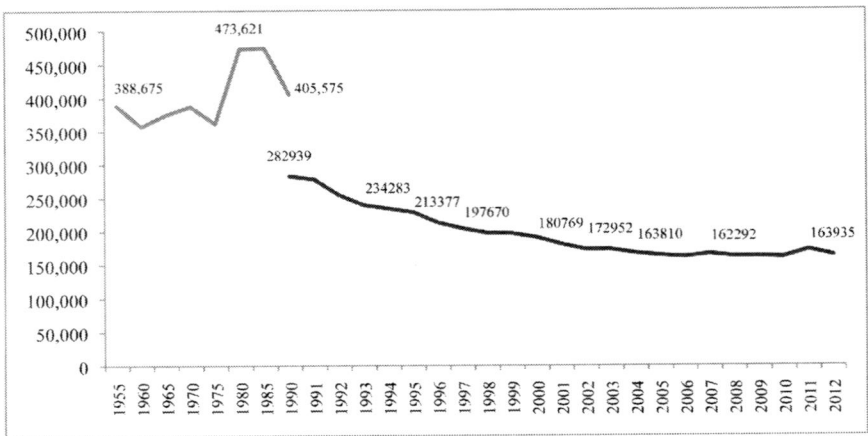

Figure 4.2.   Party membership. All parties 1955–2012.[10]

The number of party members is usually presented in the reports to the National Party congresses. These figures are often not reliable, and become even less reliable the further back in time we go (Heidar 2015). Reported Norwegian membership data differ according to the principles and practices used for generating them. In the early post-war decades, there were gaps in the time series of these figures, if at all presented. It is impossible to present historically accurate figures for party membership in Norway, as they do not exist.[11] Nevertheless, even though the membership figures are approximate, they still reflect rough changes and differences. The period from 1990 and onwards is the most accurate, as the source material has become more precise.

The total party membership from the mid-1950s until the mid-1970s holds a fairly stable level between 350,000 and 400,000 members. There are party-specific changes within this period, but no general party member trend.[12] These figures are based on nominal membership, and cannot be directly compared to the individual dues-paying membership figures for the period 1990–2012. The gap is illustrated by the 1990 figures: 400,000 nominal members compared to 280,000 individuals, a difference of 120,000 altogether. The total membership changes from 1990 to 2012 show a general decline. The 280,000 membership in 1990 is reduced to 160,000 members in 2012, which means that the parties have lost more than 40 percent of their membership in two decades. Consequently, and however shaky the actual numbers, there is little doubt that party membership in general has decreased substantially over the last 20–30 years in Norway.

Figure 4.3 shows the percentage change in party membership for all parties combined and for the individual parties. In total, there has been a 42 percent decrease in party membership from 1990 to 2012. There are some differences between the

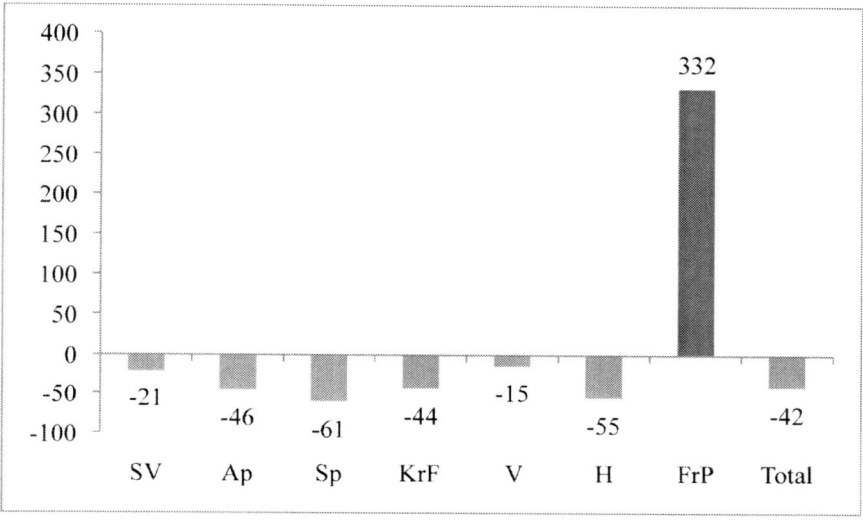

Figure 4.3.   Percentage change in party membership per party 1990–2012.[13]

parties. The percentage decrease is greatest in the four "old" parties—Centre, the Conservatives, Labour, and the Christian People's Party. The two "new" parties (the Left Socialist and the Progress), as well as the reunited Liberal party (split in the 1970s, reunited in 1988) managed either to keep their membership level roughly or actually increased their membership substantially, as in the case of the Progress Party. Nonetheless, these are minor or medium-sized parties numbering between 8,000 and 20,000 members.

In table 4.2, we compare the members registered by the party organization, with the membership calculated on the basis of voter surveys. The surveys seem to inflate the membership numbers. In nearly all years, there is an over-reporting of voters claiming membership in parties. Voters may think they are members (through the trade unions) and have forgotten to pay the dues, or they find it "inappropriate" not to be a party member. As the parties make their files increasingly more accurate, the over-reporting in surveys increased. The membership files would have increased by more than 50 percent after the 1990s had all the voters reporting membership actually been members.

Nevertheless, as reflected also in surveys, there is a decline of registered party members as percent of the total electorate. The figures varied between 13 percent and 16 percent in the years from 1965 to 1989. In the following period, survey-reported membership declined from 7 to 5 percent from 1993 to 2009. This is still high in a comparative perspective, and places Norway in the top third within the European list provided by van Biezen, Mair, and Poguntke (2012, 28).

Table 4.2.   Party members (PM) in Norway 1965–2012ª

Year	Registered PM in '000	Registered PM as % of the Electorate	PM According to Survey (%)	Estimated Number of PM According to Survey in '000	Deviation: Registered PM-Survey Estimated PM (%)
1965	375	16	16	385	+3
1969	383	15	16	413	+8
1973	358	13	17	457	+28
1977	398	14	16	445	+12
1981	457	15	17	511	+12
1985	476	15	15	465	–2
1989	416	13	13	415	–0
1993	240	7	10	326	+35
1997	204	6	10	331	+62
2001	181	5	8	267	+48
2005	164	5	8	274	+67
2009	162	5	7	247	+52
2012	164	—	—	—	—

Sources: Registered members: 1965–1989/Svåsand 1992; 1993–2012. See table 4.5. The voter surveys on membership are reported in the National Election Studies.[b]

a. The membership data before and after 1990 are not comparable. See text discussing figure 4.1. Percent change in total registered membership: 1965–1989: +11, 1993–2012: –32, 1965–2012: –56.

b. http://www.nsd.uib.no/nsddata/serier/valgundersokelser_enkeltfiler.html.

INCREASE IN PUBLIC FINANCE

The next key variable to map is public finance of parties, an institutional change that is widely assumed to have made it easier for the leadership to ignore the opinions of the (remaining) members. It should be noted that this was obviously not the rationale behind the introduction of public finance for Norwegian parties. In fact, it is quite the contrary. It was argued that the parties were important instruments to increase participation, and that public finance would make them more effective in terms of creating new, citizen-based policy programs, and more effective in presenting alternatives to the voters (Svåsand 1994c; Pierre, Svåsand, and Widfeldt 2000).[14]

At the national level, the Storting parliamentary groups received support in terms of secretarial assistance from the mid-1950s. In the 1960s, support was also given to the groups for the parliament's budget. In 1970, the Storting set up a general scheme for the public subvention of external party organizations—first, the national party, and later, the youth parties for information to work and study groups inside parties. In addition, the party organizations in the counties and municipalities now receive public support. Public subvention today is given to registered parties taking part in elections, although they must be supported by a minimum 2.5 percent of voters (at Storting elections) to qualify for basic allowance. The major part of the total state support is distributed proportionally according to the number of votes.[15] This system handicaps very small and newly established parties competing for votes.

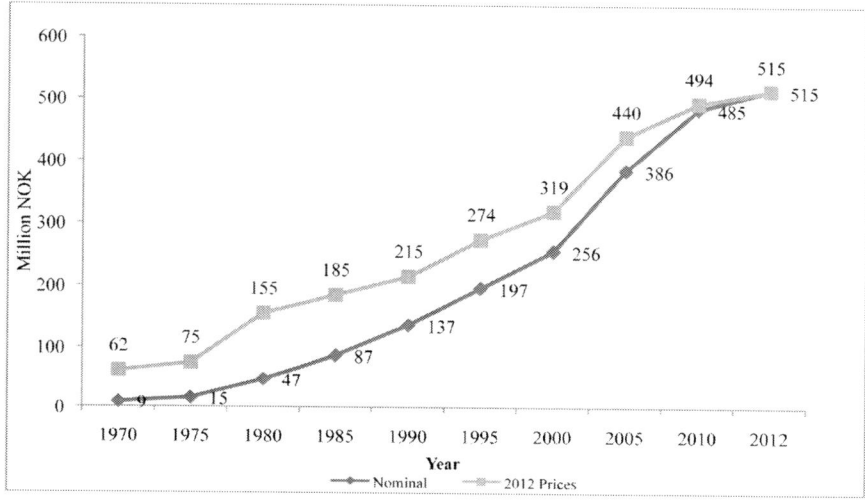

Figure 4.4. Total sum of state subventions (million NOK) to Norwegian parties 1970–2012, nominal and adjusted figures. *Source: Yearly budgets as adopted by Parliament.*[16]

In figure 4.4, we note a steep and continuous increase in public subvention to parties from 1970 to 2012 both in nominal support and in sums adjusted for inflation. Table 4A.3 in the appendix shows that public subsidies have increased from 62 to 515 million NOK from 1970 to 2012 (i.e., by over 800 percent since 1970). The increase since 1990 is 240 percent, from 215 to 515 million kroner (roughly from 27 to 65 million euro at a rate of eight NOK for one euro). The real figures are even higher, as the table does not include public finance distributed at the regional and local levels. Substantial support is given at both levels to party political activities. In other words, there is little doubt that political parties in Norway have received a rising subsidy from the state over the last four decades. Does this mean they have developed to mainly rely on state money?

Table 4.3 shows that between 2005 and 2008, the parties received between 60 and 90 percent of their income from the state. There are, however, no figures available to cover the entire period from 1970 onwards. Svåsand has shown that public finance, as a share of the national party budgets, was between 40 and 50 percent in the period from 1970 to 1990 (Svåsand 1994c, 203). Given that public support to party organizations commenced in 1970 and has subsequently risen, there is little doubt that the parties' state dependency has increased over the years. The parties certainly have other sources of income—membership fees, lotteries, and donations from individuals or organizations (e.g., trade unions, and the likes). Above all, even if the corporate membership is history, the trade unions still make huge contributions to the Labour Party's organization and election campaigns (Allern 2010b). The substantial union support gives the Labour party a lower than average state dependency in the 2000s.

The least dependent party seems to be the Conservative Party. This was also the case *after* the employers' *Confederation of Norwegian Enterprise* ended their party support in 2005 (in practice, this benefitted the Conservative Party). That said all parties receive a dominant share of their finances from the state today.

Table 4.3.   Public share of party budgets 2005–2011[a]

Party	2005	2006	2007	2008	2009	2010	2011
Socialist Left	79	82	74	74	70	77	68
Labour	64	74	71	70	70	78	62
Centre Party	62	72	80	79	68	75	68
Christian People's Party	66	70	64	68	67	61	59
Liberal Party	70	81	74	76	72	75	68
Conservative Party	52	67	62	61	64	63	68
Progress Party	89	91	83	89	83	90	90
All parties	69	77	73	74	71	74	69

Source: Statistics Norway.

a. The parties' reports on their income in accordance with the Party Law (state support, members' fees, private donations, and other income).

In the comparative research on party finance, Norway is placed among the countries with insignificant private and significant public finances (Koss 2011, 18). Other countries in this group are the other Nordic countries, along with Belgium and Austria. On the opposite end of the spectrum—countries with insignificant public and significant private finance—we find Britain, the United States, Switzerland, and Ireland. Again, the Norwegian setting could be expected to have clearly stimulated decline of the parties' representative capacity.[17]

With these basic facts in mind, we can now turn to the other main internal factors that were singled out for more scrutiny in chapter 2 as they may directly influence the parties' representative capacity beyond the party competition for votes: the system for candidate/MP selection and party discipline on public office, and the formal organizational structures of parties.

CANDIDATE SELECTION AND PARTY DISCIPLINE

Elections to the *Storting* are based on proportional representation (PR) in the country's 19 multi-member districts, with district magnitude differing from four to 19 seats. This way, the Norwegian election system opens up for ticket balancing by parties, a feature that might affect the social and political representativeness of MPs positively. Candidate selection for the party lists is the result of closed party conventions at the county level, and there is no possibility for voters to influence the rank ordering of candidates (Narud 2008). The parties control the selection of candidates more strongly than in any other Nordic country. It is virtually impossible for independent individuals and loosely organized groups to run for office.

The requirements of the Nomination Act of 1920, which prescribes a decentralized, representative selection process, were not mandatory. Nonetheless, parties had to abide by the rules to get their expenses covered by the state. Even though these rules have since been abolished, semi-decentralized decision-making remains the norm in Norway, making the county parties the decisive arena for parliamentary nominations (Valen, Narud, and Skare 2002). Lack of ballots and primaries make balanced party lists in terms of social background more likely (see chapter 2), and might temper the extent to which parties recruit MPs in a less representative manner than before. What do studies of the selection processes—the Storting nominations—tell?

Above all, empirical studies show that political experience is virtually an absolute requirement. Otherwise, the party candidate lists have for long been balanced based on criteria, like experience from local and provincial government, territorial affiliation, gender, age, political views (beyond the party program), social background, and to some extent, organizational affiliations (Valen 1988; Valen, Narud, and Skare 2002). Efficient media handling and communicational skills have become more important for political recruitment over time (Narud and Valen 2007b, 78; Allern, Karlsen, and Narud 2014). As a consequence, it could be that new selection criteria are emphasized at the expense of more traditional ones (Allern, Karlsen, and Narud 2014). That said, the party-controlled candidate selection still nurtures a high level of party discipline in the legislature (Jensen 2000), keeping party MPs in line with the party program. This makes major differences between the policy views of voters, party members/delegates, and MPs less likely despite increased social differences between the same groups.

THE FORMAL STRUCTURE OF PARTY ORGANIZATIONS

Social and political representativeness can also be colored by the extra-parliamentary party organizations. Voters' social background and political opinions can be reflected in party members and activists, and these characteristics and policy views can be channeled through the party into the parliamentary groups. If party members have become different from voters, the hypothesized decline of intra-party democracy might temper the effect of these biases in parties' (MPs) representative capacity in public office. Before turning to actual patterns of participation and influence in the next chapter, we need to examine how Norwegian parties have developed as formal organizational structures since the 1970s. To what extent are they designed for bottom-up influence today compared to the golden era of the mass party model?

With regard to *the status of party membership*, it is a matter of both obligations and rights (Heidar 2015). The parties' members must accept the general political principles of their chosen party. In the Labour Party, they must accept the statutes and the party's goals, while the Progress Party states that members must adhere to the party's goals, general principles, and political strategy. All but one party have also included in their rules that the member cannot be a member of another party. However, this is in no doubt taken for granted by the Christian People's Party as well. The Conservative and the Centre Party statutes state that a member cannot be nominated for office by another party. Some parties have explicit clauses on why and how to exclude members from the organization (Labour, Centre, Conservative, and Progress parties). Others manage without, or explicitly reject such clauses. Formal rules contribute to making the members' political preferences in line with the party's policies in fundamental terms. On their rights and obligations, however, we may first note that there is no trace in the statutes of obligations for ordinary members, excepting, of course, that disloyal behavior may lead to expulsion in some parties. Some parties explicitly state that to exercise these rights, the member must have paid the fees.

In terms of *formal power structures*, few radical changes have been observed internally and externally since the 1960s (Heidar and Saglie 2002; Allern and Saglie 2012; Allern and Karlsen 2014a). In all parties, members join "the party," but are generally expected to sign up with a local branch. Local branches are connected with the central organization through the regional units. Together, they are linked through an organizational structure with the bi- or annual party congress as the supreme body. The national leadership usually consists of a national council (*landsstyret*) and a national executive committee (*sentralstyret*), but the degree of territorial representation varies. The archetypal example has been Labour, but eventually, all major Norwegian parties developed basically similar membership organizations (Svåsand 1994a, 327; Svåsand 1994b). This means that Norwegian parties, as implied in their statutes, all have a strong degree of formal vertical integration (Allern and Saglie 2012).

With regard to the overall direction of decision-making, whether the party leadership is elected, and to what degree the national leaders are controlled by subunits, the standard finding in the literature is that representative democracy is a major organizational feature of all Norwegian parties (Heidar and Saglie 2003b; Heidar 2014). The local branch adopts motions and elects candidates for county party meetings and nomination caucuses, which again adopt motions and elect representatives to the national level. Two of the parties (Left Socialist and Christian People's) also give the right of ordinary members to present proposals directly to the national party congress, which decides on party programs.

The county branches select most of the delegates to the congress, in addition to most of the members of the national council. Members of the national-level executive (central) committee, on the other hand, do not represent county branches. These bodies are elected by the congresses although they also include members of collateral organizations, such as youth organizations. In short, Norwegian party statutes describe a high degree of *bottom-up* control. At the same time, they give municipal branches minimal *direct* say over national party affairs. Their potential influence is indirect via the county branch. This makes the county a crucial nexus in Norwegian parties, though it should be noted that the county branch is weak in resources and basically coordinates the flow of policies and resources, upwards from the local branch parties and downwards from the national party (Allern and Saglie 2012).

Direct intra-party democracy has been discussed, and most parties open up to the possibility of binding or consultative membership referenda. However, the use of ballots is a rare practice in Norwegian parties. The first (and only) time it was held, a consultative referendum on leadership selection was in the Left Socialist Party in 2012. In other words, the formal empowerment of rank-and-file members at the expense of the mid-level elite activists, as seen in some other European countries,[18] is evident only to a very limited extent (Heidar and Saglie 2002; Allern and Karlsen 2014a). The chain of delegation and accountability associated with the mass party model still enjoys high levels of legitimacy among party members and activists (Saglie and Heidar 2004).

How centralized are major national policy decisions according to party statutes? Do local parties have a significant decision-making role, or do they simply implement detailed policies developed by national elites? First, we may note that the national party manifesto and various policy resolutions are adopted by the national party congress. The potential for bottom-up influence is strong as the party congresses are basically composed of delegates based in the local, municipal party branches. It is also common to invite local parties to comment on the program proposals before the congresses (Allern 2010b, 10). Moreover, national party manifestos are fairly detailed (Green-Pedersen 2007) and regarded as binding for party representatives in public office at all levels. In all, but with the partial exception of two parties (Conservatives and Christian People's Party), the statutes prescribe loyalty to the manifesto to a greater or lesser extent. However, they do not contain guidelines for all kinds of decisions, and may be deliberately vague regarding particular issues. This could cause centralization as it gives the parliamentary party group greater leeway (Heidar 2000).

That said, today's party politics is increasingly played out in the mass media. Party headquarters and parliamentary groups have been professionalized (Rommetvedt 2003, 59; Karlsen 2010). As a consequence—and in the wake of a series of weak minority governments—there is little doubt that politics have gradually become more centered on the parliamentary activity and party leadership in Norway, as in other established democracies (Heidar and Koole 2000). Moreover, in many parties, the distinction between the central organization and its surroundings has become blurred because the early stages of their internal manifesto-making have been opened up to external participants. Interest groups have also started to spread their donations across a wider range of parties, and they have contacts not only with traditional party allies (Allern 2010b; Rommetvedt 2005, 759).

Modern technology offers virtual debating forums on party web pages and intranet. Norwegian parties resemble most parties in western democracies in their relatively conservative use of this technology (Pedersen and Saglie 2005; Karlsen 2009). However, influenced by the Obama campaign, parties, especially the Labour Party, saw more advantages to using the technology. Technology offers opportunities

for horizontal organization transcending geographical county borders, and the party
has ambitions to implement the technology in most aspects of party organization.
Although most parties reap benefits of the new technology in terms of communication, evidence of actual organizational change is limited so far (Karlsen 2013).

To sum up, there is a well-defined and statute-based membership role in Norwegian parties, which is a part of an elaborate representative decision-making system
through which members can make their voices heard. Formally, party membership
organizations in Norway carry on more or less as usual, despite decline of membership figures and increased state finance. Furthermore, even the Progress Party, which
started out as a very atypical party, ended in the 2000s in much the same way as
the mainstream parties (Jupskås 2015). In the 1970s and 1980s, the Progress Party
was a loose organization bound together by a strong party leader and populist type
opposition to the established parties, while the organization was weak at all levels.
After a dramatic schism with a split of the parliamentary group in 1993, the party
was rebuilt on a strong organizational basis, very similar to the other Norwegian
parties in organizational terms. The Socialist Left, originally a party modelled on
strong participatory values, has also become more mainstream-like over time, with
a representative structure and strong party leaders (Allern 2010b). The question is
if structural stability and convergence have tempered the changes in direction of the
less influential party grass roots.

THE DATA MATERIAL

The data we shall employ for the subsequent studies of activity, influence, and congruence consist of a significant number of surveys of voters, members, delegates, and
MPs, which have been collected by a number of different researchers and research
projects. We use data related to (roughly) three points in time: 1990, 2000, and
2010. Ideally, we should have had surveys back to the 1970s, but what we have at
least covers the period when changes might for sure be expected. We also rely on
other data sources, and the details on these, as well as on the surveys, will be given
in the relevant empirical chapters. Table 4.4 gives an overview of all the surveys used
in the book.

To study party membership activity, we mainly use surveys of party members
(chapter 5). To study descriptive congruence, we use the surveys on voters, members,
and delegates, as well as biographical data on MPs (chapter 6). To study political
congruence, we use surveys on voters, members, delegates, and MPs (chapter 7).

The national election studies (NES) are used to map changes in the electorate over
time. The election studies are based on large representative samples and have been
conducted regularly for every parliamentary election since 1964 (Valen and Aardal
1994). In addition, we use a representative national survey conducted in 2009 by
our research group,[19] which includes several questions identical to the ones included
in the member, delegate, and MP surveys.

Table 4.4. Data used to map changes in parties' representative capacity 1990–2010[a]

	Voters	Members	Delegates	MPs
1990	NES 1989 (N=2195, 73%) NES 1993 (N=2194, 74%)	Member survey 1991 (N=1879, 68%)	No survey	MP Survey 1988 (N=147, 94%) MP Survey 1993 (N=128, 78%) MP Biographies 1989–93
2000	NES 2001 (N=2052, 70%)	Member survey 2000 (N=1721, 61%)	Delegate survey 2000 (N=1357, 71%)	MP Survey 2000 (N = missing) and MP Survey 2005 (N=116, 68%) MP Biographies 2001–05
2010	NES 2009 (N=1782, 61%) and Citizen survey 2009 (N=989)	Member survey 2009 (N=3314, 49%)	Delegate survey 2009 (N=907, 55%)	MP Survey 2012 (N=116, 68%) MP Biographies 2009–13

a. Number of respondents and response rates in parentheses. NES = National Election Study.

Table 4.5. The surveys: N's by party 1990–2010[a]

	1990				2000				2010				
	V	M	D	MPs[b]	V	M	D	MPs	V[c]	V[d]	M	D	MPs
SV	135	335	n.a.	17	236	295	154	17	120	80	581	116	6
Ap	683	281	n.a.	48	357	268	221	30	504	244	428	179	39
Sp	316	285	n.a.	9	93	227	148	5	97	28	455	119	5
KrF	126	286	n.a.	8	245	231	181	15	67	56	440	115	7
V	62	260	n.a.	n.a.	70	277	139	n.a.	66	36	487	119	n.a.
H	278	213	n.a.	27	428	198	187	29	291	100	458	147	25
FrP	82	220	n.a.	18	170	225	131	18	280	155	465	112	32

a. National Election Study (NES) 1993.
b. MP Survey 1993.
c. National Election Study.
d. Citizen survey.

The party member survey has been undertaken three times: in 1991, 2000, and 2009, while the delegate survey was carried out twice: in 2000 and 2009 (Heidar 1994; Heidar and Saglie 2002; Jupskås 2009). The membership surveys comprise a random sample from the parties' membership files: 400 for each party in 1991 and 2000, and 1000 for each party in 2009. All delegates to the Norwegian party's national congress in 2000/01 and 2009 (ranging between 192 and 300 in 2000/01 and between 195 and 230 people in 2009) were included in the delegate survey.

We look at five surveys of MPs carried out in 1988, 1993, 2000, 2005, and 2012. By including all five surveys, we maximize the number of available identical policy questions (we return to this aspect in chapter 7). The surveys were sent to all members of the parliament and the response rate is generally very good (see table 4.4).[20] In table 4.5, we present the N's by party in all these surveys, as we do not have the space to include these in all our tables.

The operationalization, measurements, and methods to be applied will be discussed in detail in the empirical chapters. To make our empirical findings robust, we adopt a multiple measurements approach (see chapters 6 and 7).

CONCLUSION

In this chapter, we have first presented the rise of the Norwegian party system and the parties to be analyzed in this book: the Socialist Left, the Labour Party, the Centre Party, the Christian People's Party, the Liberals, the Conservatives, and the Progress Party. Subsequently, we have described the patterns of competition among these parties and presented the major issues on which they attract voters. We have shown that cleavage-based party competition and continuous ideological differences mean that parties still offer voters real alternatives on the election day. Multiple parties compete for votes and may cater to different constituencies.

Next, we looked at the key organizational factors in the literature predicting the decline of parties' representative capacity: decaying membership and increasing state dependency. There is no doubt that these factors apply to Norwegian parties as well. There has been a major decline in party membership from 1990 to 2012. The figures have dropped from 280,000 to 160,000 individual, dues-paying members—a decline of more than 40 percent. The decline has been even greater from the peak years in the mid-1980s, but we do not have very reliable figures from these years. There are differences between the parties, however, as the so-called "new parties," the Left Socialist and Progress parties, both increased their membership—the latter with 60 percent—after 2000. In the same period, the public finance of parties increased substantially. It more than doubled in five years from 1975 to 1980, then increased by more than 50 percent in real value every decade after. Hence, we may conclude that the Norwegian case is highly relevant for studying the consequences of mass party decline for representation. Norwegian parties have been stimulated to move away from voters since the 1970s and 1980s.

At the same time, we have demonstrated that both the Norwegian political system and the parties have some features that do not necessarily point in the same negative direction. First, proportional elections open up for ticket balancing, and closed nominations mean that party organizations may control the candidate selection. Second, extensive party programs and strong party organizations keep MPs in line. Finally, the survival of the mass party's formal structure might have tempered the marginalization of party activists, vis-à-vis party elites. We will get back to all these aspects when discussing the results of the empirical assessment that follows next, based on the data material finally presented above.

APPENDIX

Table 4A.1.   Party membership in Norwegian Parties, 1950–2004

				Party				
Year	Socialist Left	Labour	Centre	Christian People's	Liberal	Conservative[a]	Progress	Total
1950	n.a.	200,501					n.a.	200,501
1955	n.a.	174,080	64,000[b]	29,000	28,000	93,595[c]	n.a.	388,675
1960	3,295[d]	165,096	61,000	30,346[e]		97,509	n.a.	357,246
1965	3,224	150,262	68,000	37,545		115,855[f]	n.a.	374,886
1970	2,437[g]	155,254	70,000	42,023[h]	13,220[i]	104,863	n.a.	387,797
1975		137,954	56,542	52,605	6,547	107,867		361,515
1980	9,500[j]	153,507	53,517	69,697	12,007	165,393	10,000[k]	473,621
1985	11,000	174,143	51,376	59,275	11,670[l]	167,063	[m]	474,527
1990	13,072	128,106	47,117	56,176	11,300	132,930	16,874[n]	405,575

Source: Demker and Svåsand (2005).

a. The numbers of members include ancillary organizations.
b. Members in 1957.
c. Members in 1956.
d. Members in 1963.
e. Members in 1961.
f. Members in 1964.
g. Members in 1971.
h. Members in 1969.
i. Members in 1972.
j. Members in 1981.
k. Members in 1981.
l. Members in 1984.
m. Data not available.
n. Members in 1989.

Table 4A.2.   Party members in Norwegian parties, 1990–2012. Paid-up members

	Socialist	Labour[a]	Centre	Christian[c]	Liberal	Cons.[b]	Progress[d]	Total[e]
1990	10,272	97,634	—	43,382	11,345	71,859	—	282,939
1991	10,086	101,211	41,655	42,484	11,398	65,074	—	278,177
1992	10,809	86,871	44,261	41,934	7,800	56,996	—	254,721
1993	11,473	77,797	43,378	40,215	7,300	53,097	4,370	239,623
1994	11,478	73,574	43,397	43,718	7,000	49,451	3,671	234,283
1995	9,318	75,017	42,668	41,756	7,000	46,154	4,976	228,884
1996	8,609	68,833	—	39,703	7,000	41,445	5,654	213,377
1997	7,696	64,415	37,606	38,845	7,491	39,477	6,816	204,343
1998	7,972	62,984	33,960	38,786	6,857	37,208	7,905	197,670
1999	—	61,327	31,626	37,311	6,852	38,761	11,224	196,800
2000	7,428	58,768	30,298	36,963	6,552	37,043	11,824	190,876
2001	7,274	52,929	26,478	37,237	5,992	36,291	12,567	180,769
2002	7,676	50,835	23,932	36,051	5,561	29,973	16,746	172,776
2003	7,751	51,672	23,570	34,741	5,609	28,767	18,839	172,952
2004	9,994	51,033	22,153	32,447	5,683	26,267	17,660	167,241
2005	10,591	51,575	20,987	31,205	5,798	24,801	16,848	163,810
2006	9,774	50,252	19,952	30,378	6,041	23,598	19,581	161,582
2007	8,499	51,163	21,080	29,804	6,968	25,482	20,961	165,964
2008	8,305	48,589	20,974	29,111	7,244	25,042	21,019	162,292
2009	8,522	50,264	17,264	28,079	8,509	24,712	22,876	162,235
2010	7,920	49,407	16,977	27,338	8,632	26,172	22,623	161,079
2011	8,380	55,869	17,636	25,075	9,523	31,301	22,310	172,105
2012	8,074	52,578	16,392	24,253	9,643	32,095	18,888	163,935

Source: The parties' yearly reports, but for Labour 1992–1995, Christian 1990–2009, and Conservative parties, the figures are estimates. See notes.

a. For Labour, the figures from 1992 to 1995 have collectively affiliated party members. See table 3A1. Self-paying members/individually paying members are estimated for this year by the known ratio self-paying members/total membership for the years 1990, 1991, and 1996. The average ratio is 0.76, and varies little over these three years (0.73–0.78).

b. The Conservatives only present figures for paying members from 2003. The figures for 1990–2002 presented in the table are estimates. First, we calculated the average ratio for paying/total membership in 2003–2010, which was 0.70, and varied between 0.69–0.72. Paying members in 1990–2003 were then estimated based on the figures on total membership.

c. Similar estimations are done for the Christian Party in 1990–2009. Here, the estimates are based on the ratio in 2010 and 2011, as these are the only two years where we have both figures. The average was 0.77. Figures for 2010, 2011, and 2012 were given by e-mail from the organizational secretary of the party. For 2011, the figures include the youth organization (KrFU). For 2012, however, only members of the Central Party organization are included.

d. The Progress Party does not judge their figures from before 1993 as reliable. The ratio paid-up/total members in this period varies significantly so that it is not reasonable to estimate the pre-1993 figures.

e. To calculate total membership, we have also estimated the figures for missing years. Socialist 1999 is the average of 1998 and 2000. Centre 1990 (total 45,000 includes the youth organization) is estimated by subtracting the estimated number of youth members. In 1996, the Centre figure is the average of 1995 and 1997. Progress Party in 1990–92 is estimated on the basis of the paid-up/total ratio 1993–95.

Table 4A.3. Total sum of state subventions to Norwegian parties, 1970–2012. Percent increase[a]

Year	Nominal in Million NOK	Adjusted to 2012 Prices in Million NOK	Increase over Last 10 Years (%)
1970	8.5	62	
1975	15.2	75	
1980	47.4	155	1970–1980: 250
1985	87.3	185	
1990	136.7	215	1980–1990: 139
1995	196.7	274	
2000	256.0	319	1990–2000: 148
2005	385.8	440	
2010	484.6	494	2000–2010: 155
2012	515.3	515	

Source: Yearly budgets as adopted by Parliament. Numbers were compiled by Jonas Tysland (1970–2010) and Peder Wahl (2011–12).

a. The figures include state support to national party organization and to the party levels and groups (county, municipal, youth, and so on), but not the support given by county and municipal authorities to the parties (organizations, as well as party groups in elected assemblies).

NOTES

1. See for example "Democracy index 2012: Democracy at a standstill," Economist Intelligence Unit. March 14, 2013. For detailed general overviews of the institutional setting of parties in Norway, see for example Strøm and Narud (2003) and Allern (2010a).

2. For a more detailed presentation of the Norwegian party system, see, e.g., Aylott (forthcoming).

3. After WWII, the Centre Party moved from the right to the left side of the middle in the political spectrum, see Narud and Valen (2007b, 148).

4. We apply the terms used in Mackie and Rose (1991) and in the Yearbook of *European Journal of Political Research*. However, it should be noted that *Kristelig Folkeparti* (KrF) itself applies the label "Christan Democratic Party," not the literal translation "Christian People's Party," see for example http://www.stortinget.no/english/alphabetic.html.

5. In 1969, the youth organization left SF (later SV) and founded a Maoist-Leninist communist party (Arbeidernes Kommunistiske Parti, AKP (m-l) in 1973. The other new parties excluded are the Coastal Party (Kystpartiet) and The Greens (Miljøpartiet De Grønne). The latter party holds, for the first time, one seat in the Storting in 2013–17.

6. The following section relies on Karlsen (2015), Karlsen and Aardal (2011), and Aardal (2015).

7. A minority coalition of the parties in the center (KrF, V, Sp) governed from 1997 to 2000.

8. The sum of all absolute changes divided by two.

9. In the statutes, there is no mention of intermediate roles of "sympathizers," "supporters," or "party friends" giving political access or rights to non-members. Members can join the main party organization, the youth party or—in several parties—special organizations for pensioners and (mostly earlier) women. They pay an annual fee varying from NOK 250 to 400 (about 30–50 euro) for members with employment. There are lower fees for youth, students, pensioners,

and others not economically active. Membership is from 13 years upwards, but the young usually sign up with the youth party. In practice, members are all connected to their local branch.

10. For details on how the figures are collected, see tables 5A.1 and 5A.2 in chapter 5.

11. First, the figures summarized the reports given by the lower organizational levels—the local branch and the county—if they file a report in the first place. The local branches based their reports on notoriously shaky membership files. Even as late as when the first survey on party members was conducted in 1991, which was based on the parties' own records, questionnaires were often returned stating that the recipient was no longer a member, that he or she was deceased, or the records included the name of a company or corporate body in the lists given by the party (Heidar and Saglie 2002). The latter indicated that to some extent, the membership file and the general mailing lists of the party were the same. It was a practice among the parties that the names were kept on file for some unspecified years, even after the members had stopped paying their fees. Another problem is that the membership numbers include different sets of members. Some include only members of the main party section, others include the auxiliary organizations like youth, women, and pensioners. However, files do not systematically present separate numbers. As noted, Labour had, until the mid-1990s, collectively affiliated trade union members. They do not always give separate numbers for these. In other words, when excavating party membership numbers back in time, we cannot find figures that compare to these.

12. See the tables in the appendix.

13. For details on how the figures are collected, see tables 4.A1 and 4.A2 in the appendix.

14. The public debate on party subsidies was at first dominated by the skeptics, particularly in the governing Labour Party. Party politics was a "private" activity and should not be mixed with state affairs. A committee preparing the general party support in 1970 found that the main argument favoring support was that the parties were necessary to uphold democratic procedures and sustain public political debates (Heidar 2014). The main arguments against it was that public means should not support political activities. The report noted the danger that parties may become dependent on the state, and that majorities could unduly favor their own parties. It was also noted that support might pacify members, increase the power of leaders and party officials, and conserve the existing party system. In other words, they included "cartel party" arguments in their warnings of the late 1960s. For many years, the Conservative and the Progress parties were, in principle, against state support. At the next main juncture, however, in a public commission in the early 2000s, all parties accepted that the parties were of fundamental importance to democratic processes and it was a legitimate public task to support their activities.

15. Ot. prp. no. 84 2004–2005; http://lovdata.no/dokument/NL/lov/2005-06-17-102, downloaded 7/12–13.

16. Adjusted figures 2012=100. The figures include *state* support to national party organizations and auxiliaries, as well as to the parliamentary party groups and to regional and local party organizations, but not the support given by county and municipal authorities to the parties (organizations as well as party groups in elected assemblies).

17. See also the studies by Scarrow (2006); Nassmacher (2009); Pierre, Svåsand, and Widfeldt (2000).

18. See for example Katz and Mair (1995) and Scarrow (2002).

19. Hanne Marthe Narud coordinated this work. The survey was carried out by TNS Gallup.

20. The various surveys were carried out by the following scholars: Matthews and Valen (1999); Gulbrandsen et al. (2002); Narud, Rasch, and Valen (2005); Heidar (1994, 2013).

5

Participation, Communication, and Influence

For party organizations to provide channeling of member opinions to the party leaders an active membership must be able to establish working contacts with the leaders and the leaders must be responsive to members' demands. As argued in chapter 2, the members should have a reasonable level of activity. There should be bottom-up communication between the rank-and-file party members and the party leaders at different levels, and the members ought to express satisfaction with the party leaders' willingness to listen to the grass roots. Activity, contact, and satisfaction do not in themselves guarantee a well-functioning intra-party democracy, but they still indicate an operative linkage mechanism inside the parties.

A central question is of course how much activity, how much contact, and how willing to listen. All should be above some minimum level, but what this minimum level is is open for discussion. Our main task here, however, is to study empirically whether there has been a decline in bottom-up party processes inside parties, as expected on the basis of general membership decline. In chapter 2, we discussed the proposition that a shrinking membership would lead to a marginalization of party members in the internal decision-making process. Here, we investigate this claim empirically, focusing on three questions: Is the level of activity declining in parties? Is there a decreasing level of contacts between the party elites and the grass roots? Do the rank-and-file members find the leadership less responsive than before?

Based on the arguments predicting decline of parties' representative capacity, we expect to find different levels of activism in the parties according to their degrees of membership loss. The members-leadership linkage is expected to become less operative in parties with high membership losses and high reliance on public finance. In the previous chapter, we showed that public finance was affecting Norwegian parties evenly. No party was markedly less dependent on public finance than the others; they had all become more dependent on state money over the years. We expect this to affect all parties equally. The membership losses and gains, however, differed between the parties.

In the chapter, we first briefly report on previous empirical research on party activism and internal party decision-making in Norway. Then, we present the time-series data on Norwegian party membership in terms of activities, internal communication, and perceived influence. Based on these data, we discuss the question of whether the party membership has become less relevant for the party leadership during the years since 1990.

PREVIOUS RESEARCH ON PARTY MEMBER
ACTIVITY AND INFLUENCE IN NORWAY

The activity level of party members and internal party democracy has been central themes in several studies on Norwegian parties, although much is not available in English.[1] Membership activity in Norway was reported to be low in the early 1990s with only 20 percent of the membership being reasonably active at meetings (Heidar 1994). In a study from 2003, it was concluded that there was no evidence that the members had become less active from 1991 to 2000, even though the total numbers of members had declined in the period (Heidar and Saglie 2003a). The study emphasized stability rather than change (see also Heidar et al. 2012). We may note that all the studies reported in 1994, 2003, and 2004 were based on the same membership data, which we present below.

There is no consensus as to whether Michel's law of oligarchy is valid for the parties, but that may have more to do with the rather vague analytical standards embedded in this approach than with the available data. A study from 2004 concluded, as mentioned in chapter 3, that the decision-making structures and practices of Duverger's mass party model prevail (Saglie and Heidar 2004, 402). The organizational structure is hierarchical, but may also ensure accountability. The members are reasonably satisfied with their leader, although at the time they were a little less so in the Labour party (403). There was little pressure from the grass roots to introduce party reforms such as leadership ballots and the like. In a more recent study on vertical integration in Norwegian parties, it is shown on the basis of surveys with local party leaders and interviews with county secretaries from 2008, that the parties' local leadership have frequent contacts with the national party: "The links between the national party and the county branches seem strong at the individual level" (Allern and Saglie 2012, 957). The authors conclude that Norwegian parties have a somewhat conflicting nature as they seem to be well-integrated, formally partly governed from below, and rather centralized, but with significant local autonomy in policy issues (ibid., 966).

PARTY MEMBER ACTIVITY

We expect that the level of party member activities has decreased significantly over the last two decades, and that parties with little or no decline of membership would be less affected. The party member surveys of 1991, 2000, and 2009 have several questions that can be used to indicate *level* and *types* of party activity. The members were first asked whether they, during the last year, had participated in any party arrangements like meetings, educational courses, seminar gatherings, and celebrations. If yes, they were asked about how many times they had participated. They were also asked whether they had taken part in a given number of activities. These covered participation in party study circles, donation of money, holding office, discussing party policies internally or externally, and so forth. Together, these two dimensions—the quantitative and the qualitative—will be our operational definition of party member activity.

In table 5.1, we see that about half of the membership in the Norwegian parties has taken part in one or more party events. It also shows that there is a slight trend toward a more active membership from 1991 to 2009. Of the very active, however, the share of members turning up for five or more such events declined from 24 percent in 1991 to 18 percent in 2009. Overall, there is a noticeable, but hardly strong trend toward increased membership activity during this period. At least it is definitely *no decline* in party activism for members in Norwegian parties.[2]

Table 5.1. Participation at party events, 1991–2009. Percent[a]

# of events	1991	2000	2009
0	53	52	48[b]
1	11	13	9
2–4	18	16	19
5–9	8	9	10
10–20	6	6	7
20+	4	4	7
N	1890	1721	3314

a. Question: Did you take part in any events last year—branch meetings, seminars, gatherings, parties? Weighted figures (N not weighted).
b. Change significant at 0.01 level.

The figures on membership change in 1990–2010 in chapter 3 show that the high decline parties were the Labour Party, Centre Party, Christian People's Party, and the Conservatives. As we showed in chapter 3, the Progress Party actually increased its membership in the period (from 1995), and the Socialist Left and the Liberal Party had moderate to low decline. If there is any connection between the decline of membership and party member activities, we should see a difference between these two groups of parties listed in the table.

Table 5.2. Party events. Changes from 1991 to 2009 for the not actives and the very actives (5+). By party. Percentage points[a]

	SV	Ap	Sp	KrF	V	H	FrP	Ap/H/ KrF/H	SV/V/ FrP
Not actives	+7*	—	–5	+9*	–3	–19**	–1	–3.8	+1
Very actives (5+)	–5	+8*	+5	–2	+3	+11**	+3	+5.5	+0.3
N 1991/	345/	281/	285/	286/	260/	213/	220/		
2009	581	428	455	440	487	458	465		

*Significant at 0.05 level.
**Significant at 0.01 level.

a. Question: Did you take part in any events last year—branch meetings, seminars, gatherings, parties? High membership decline parties in bold.

The results shown in table 5.2 are not in line with these expectations. Here, we look only at those not participating at all and compare those to the highly active taking part in five or more events (in the appendix we show the figures for all levels in table 5A.1). Three of the four parties with a high membership decline (bold in table 5.2) have a rise in high-activity members and a reduction in passive members. On the other hand, the parties with less membership decline have a small rise in both inactive and high-activity members.

Table 5.3. Party members, all and active, in percentage of the electorate 1991–2009

	Electorate '000	Party members '000	Party members as percentage of electorate	No. of party members participating in at least one party event '000	Percentage of electorate that participated in at least one party event
1993	3.260	240	7.4	113	3.5
2001	3.360	181	5.4	87	2.6
2009	3.500	162	4.6	84	2.5

Sources: Statistics Norway, tables 4.2 and 5.1.

The only parties matching the expectations are the Christian Party (both decline in membership and member activity) and the Progress Party (rising membership and rising activity), although the changes are small and not significant. The Conservative Party (membership declining) had a clear turn toward a more active membership. Some, but not all of these changes are sufficiently large to be statistically significant. At any rate, looking at the surveys on party members, there is clearly *no support for the suggestion that declining membership leads to less active members at the level of individual parties.*

There is an important supplement to this conclusion, however. When referring to increasing member activity, we only refer to the party members *at any given time.*

When the number of party members decreases, even a rising internal activism may not stem the tide toward a decline in the *overall party activism* among the voters. Looking at the macro-level figures presented in table 5.3, this is precisely what we find: a decline in overall party activism in the electorate as a whole. Here, we estimate the share of active party members in the citizenry as a whole. The percentage for those who signed up as party members has declined from 7 to 4 percent in the period (cf. chapter 3). Based on the party member surveys, the share of active members in the electorate, modestly defined as members participating in at least one party event last year, has dropped from 3.5 to 2.5 percent over 20 years, in spite of some increased activism on the part of remaining members. Intuitively, this makes sense: when the parties lose members, the least active leaves the party first. In terms of absolute numbers, those active in parties has dropped from 113,000 to 84,000.

Table 5.4. Participation in party activities during the last year, and holding party or public office (percentage)[ab]

	1991	2000	2009	Change (1991– 2009)
Internal activities				
Discussed with other party members	21	21	37	+16*
Addressed a party meeting or wrote letters to the press	5	7	16	+11*
Participated in the preparation of motions within the party	9	12	15	+6*
Participated in a study circle arranged by the party	9	8	9	—
Member of executive committee in local branch				
Held other office in local branch	11	9	13	+2
External activities				
Discussed the party's policies with non-members[c]	n.a.	55	63	+8*
Worked for the party in the last election campaign	30	34	37	+7*
Took part in demonstrations etc.	11	13	15	+4*
Wrote in the press	6	8	12	+6*
Was member or deputy member of the municipal council	9	12	17	+8*
Was member of a municipal committee	15	13	17	+2
Financial support				
Donated money to party funds or election funds	26	24	22	–4*
N not weighted	1890	1721	3314	

*Significant at 0.01 level.

a. Several questions, generally on the following format: Below, there is a list of various party activities. Please fill in the boxes if you have taken part in any of these activities during the last year.
b. N is weighted to calculate the figures for all party members. Weighted N's were 1879 (1991), 1721 (2000), and 3315 (2009).
c. Test of magnificance, 2000–2009.

So far, we have only presented the quantitative side to party activism. In table 5.4, we look at different types of party activism—internal, external, and the financial. The overall change is toward a rise, or levelling, in all the activities with one exception. The exception is the decline of four percentage points in the share donating money to their party. On the other hand, and more in line with the general picture, there is a steep rise of 16 percentage points—from 21 percent in 1991 to 37 percent in 2009—for members discussing issues and candidates with other party members. The share of members that addressed a party meeting or wrote letters in the press rose from 5 percent to 16 percent, while the share of members taking part in study circles remain at the same level (i.e., 9 percent). Looking at external activities, members' participation in the election campaigns increased from 30 to 37 percent over the same period. In all parties, we find that members are active as party ambassadors, advocating the party policies to non-members. This increased after 2000, covering 63 percent for Norwegian party members in 2009. Which activities are the most demanding is not necessarily clear; demanding in terms of time or qualifications would be one question for this discussion. There is, however, an increasing share of members taking on internal and external office, as well as preparing motions for the party debate.

Do we find differences between parties according to trends in membership decline? Nearly all the activities increased or roughly stayed at the same level (see table 5A.2 in the appendix). The strongest decline is found for the members of the Left Socialists (SV) when asked about participation in study circles. The score declined from 15 to 4 percent (not shown in the table) with a net loss of 11 percentage points. There is also a decline in the donation of money to the parties, except for the Conservative Party members. Again, dividing the parties into "high decline" and "rise/stability" does not confirm the expectation that membership decline triggers lower activity among party members. Apart from the fact that nearly all activities have been on the rise, the increase is essentially larger for high decline parties in most areas, most likely because these parties had a larger group of "not actives" leaving the party. Two minor exceptions to this are found in responses to "discussing issues and candidates with other party members" and "membership in municipal councils."

Summing up, there are *few signs that levels of party member activities have declined in the 1991–2009 period.* On the contrary, the remaining members actually increase their activities in most fields. There are also no tendencies for more demanding types of activism to decrease the most, or at least increase less. Yet again, the share of *voters* being active on these party arenas is in decline.

COMMUNICATION

The party can only channel member preferences to party representatives in public office if there are, first, active members, and second, an internal process of communication between members and leaders. Declining membership and marginalized members would presumably lead to members' opinions being less important for the party leadership. They would turn to other potentially more significant sources on grass roots' opinions to check policy matters, turning to the voters and other civil society organizations and movements that could impact their chances of re-election. On the basis of the "decline of parties" arguments, we therefore expect that *the extent of contact between different levels in the parties has decreased notably over the last two decades.*

Allern and Saglie (2012, 967) found that the formal organizational links are still supplemented by "a significant informal web of intra-party links" by means of regular contacts among office holders at different party levels. Given that close to half of the membership never turn up for the party arrangements, we would not expect much communication between party grass roots and elites. Our first measure of internal, "bottom-up" party communication is the share of members confirming that they have contacted their party's representatives in public office to promote a particular policy position. Our second measure is whether the party membership has an interest in issues going beyond the local affairs into national and international policy issues, thereby indicating an interest in participating in the national party debates. Moreover, in terms of communication, we would expect that declining, old membership parties experienced less and decreasing communication between members and leaders. Member retreat into local politics would indicate a decline of the party organization as a members' channel to impact the party MPs.

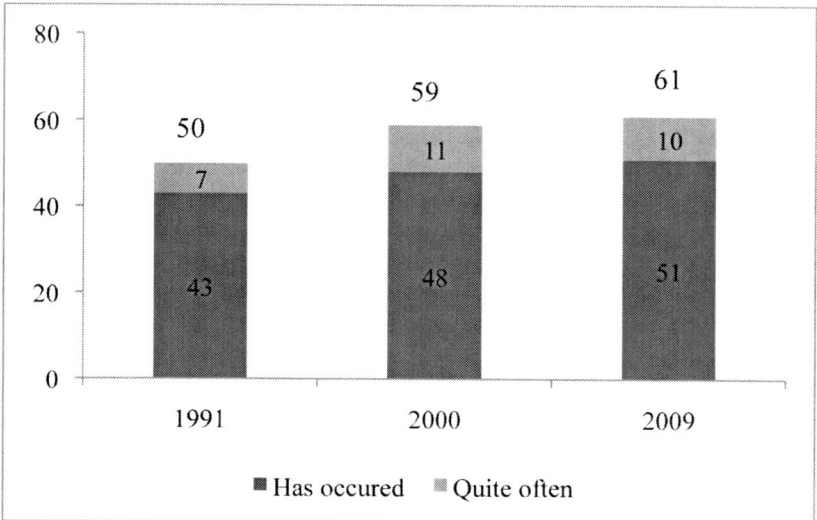

Figure 5.1. Proportion of members that has contacted party representatives in public office.[3]

A substantial part of the membership—almost 40 percent in 2009—has never contacted their representatives in public office to influence his or her position on an issue (figure 5.1). On the other hand, five to six out of 10 actually do make such contact, with one of these contacting "quite often." We can also note that there is a significant rise in member contacts during the period covered. In total, there is a rise of 11 percentage points. In the period with decline of membership, there has been a rise in contacts.

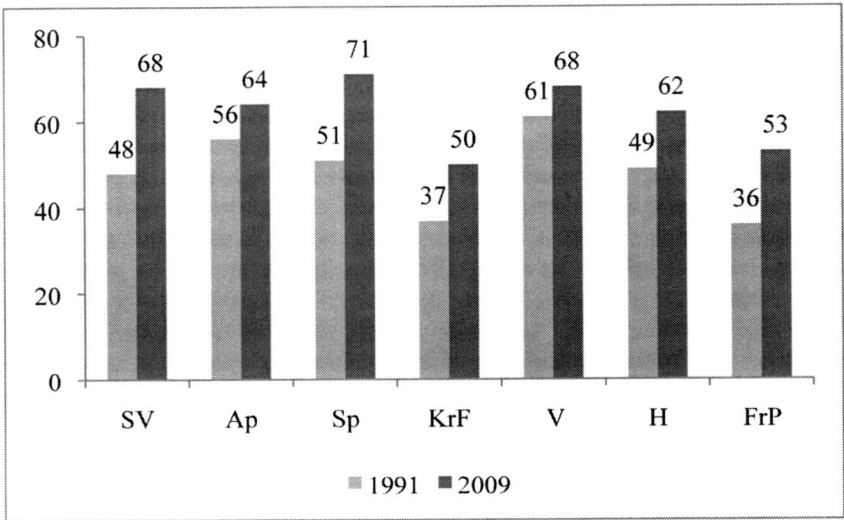

Figure 5.2. Share of members that have contacted the party's representatives in public office 1991 and 2009 by party.[4]

We find no sign that the "decline parties" are less part of this rising contacts pattern (figure 5.2). The rise in contact pattern is only marginally more manifest in the stable/no decline parties compared to the others. The individual party differences are much more noticeable, with a high rise in the Left Socialists and the Centre parties. However, these changes cut across the decline vs. stable parties' distinction. Some alternative explanations of a more contextual nature are tempting: both the SV and the Centre Party were out of government in 1991, but part of the government in 2009. This difference could explain why the members found contact more attractive, or beneficial, in 2009. Another high rise party, the Progressive Party, also had much broader public representation in 2009 than in 1991. This may be the decisive difference between these parties, not their loss or gain of membership. For the Centre Party, we may also see the same concentration of an active membership, as the less dedicated members left the party.

We need to check if the members' political interests are mainly confined to the local party alone, or whether they also have a more general political interest. Moreover, the surveys do not differentiate between leadership at different levels of the organization, meaning that "contacts" could indicate local links, as well as national contacts. Are member-leadership contacts primarily about local issues at the local level, or is national and international politics also on the members' horizon? Party members may nurture and cultivate their political interests in local party milieus, but they may also work to influence county or national party policies. Local party organizations may promote local democracy by creating a meeting ground for members and local bosses. At the other extreme, local branches could organize networks for national contacts through which party members can influence national-level decisions. We will argue that to sustain the representative capacity of parties in a political system like Norway's, members with interests at both the local and the national levels are needed. In addition, a decline in national and/or international interest would contribute to a marginalization of members.

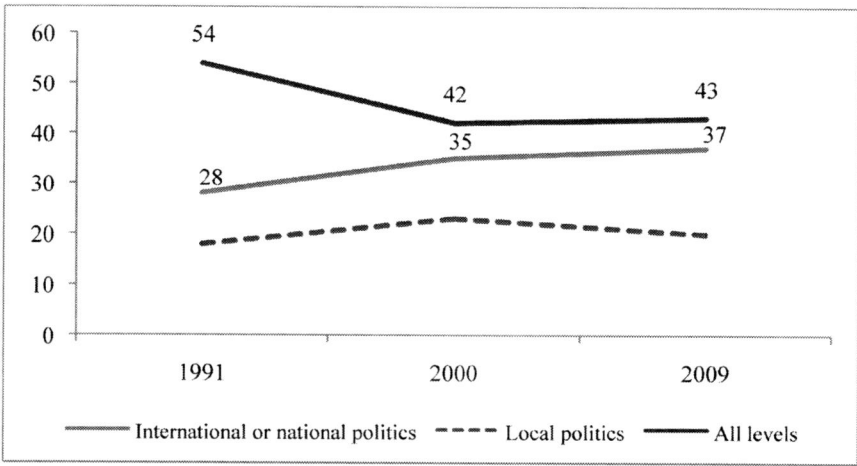

Figure 5.3. Proportion of members most concerned with politics at the national level, with international politics, and about equally concerned with all levels.[5]

In figure 5.3, we see that a majority of members are interested in both local and national politics. Fifty-four percent had this dual interest in 1991. Forty-three percent had this dual interest in 2009. Even though the party members are organized within local party branches, they are not politically bounded by the local setting. At all three points in time, we find more members that are primarily concerned with national and international politics rather than with politics at the local level. More important in our analysis here is that there has been a significant rise in the share of members that focus primarily on the national and international levels. The percentage increased from 28 to 37 in the period. We see from table 5A.3 in the appendix that the rise is particularly notable in the Labour, Centre, Christian, and the Liberal parties. This does not give a reason to believe that specific organizational trends in terms of membership decline and increase in public subvention or party age for that matter have something to do with vertical contact patterns within parties. Obviously, local claims may trigger and require national policy decisions, and it is no great surprise that members are interested in more than their local arena. A general trend toward closer integration of party branches and levels, the centralization of the media, and the domination of national politicians can account for these changes, making the political horizons of the party members more similar. The profile of member interest reveals that there is a strong basis for bottom-up processes—with local, as well as national foci—inside all parties.

In conclusion, there is *no support in these data for the proposition that contact between different party levels has decreased over time.* The opposite seems to be the case. We have also seen that the memberships have their enduring political focus at both the local and the national/international level, making the party linkage cross-level and national. In addition, we have not found support for the hypothesis that decreasing contact patterns can primarily be found among the parties with a declining membership.

INFLUENCE

Our third indicator for internal party linkage after activity and contact is influence. Do the party members influence decisions in their parties? How do they perceive their own influence? Has their influence decreased as the party declined in membership? On the base of the "decline of parties" arguments, we would expect that *the perceived member influence on party decision-making has decreased significantly over the last two decades.* Clearly, we would have preferred indicators for actual influence, but like any power study, analyzing party decisions is a very complex matter (Cross and Katz 2013). In our measurement of influence, we rely on the perceptions of the party members themselves. Such perceptions may be distorted, but we expect that differences in levels of perceived impact—over time and between parties—will also reflect realities. Of course, one may imagine that groups can be under the spell of "false consciousness," culturally induced distortions, and the like, but we expect that the voluntary work within parties in free democracies are less likely settings for such developments.

In table 5.5, we first look at members' perceptions of party decision-making and grass-root influence at the *local* level. Most members state that it is "difficult to say" or they do not give an opinion. There are, however, about 40 percent giving an answer, and these members are divided evenly in groups stating that the leadership "gets its way most of the time," and those who say that the members "occasionally win, even against the wishes of the leadership." The change from 1991 to 2009 is that more members believe that the member can influence the leadership. About one in four in 2009 was of the opinion that the leadership had to follow the members instead of the other way around. At the least, this indicates an *open* process in local issues. Many members are, as noted, without an opinion, but these are predominantly the non-active members, members without experience from recent party decision-making.[6] We can add that this is clearly not unexpected that the leadership gets its

Table 5.5. Impression on the chance of an ordinary member winning the local party branch over own point of view. Percent[a]

	1991	*2000*	*2009*	*1991– 2009*
The leadership gets its way most of the time	19	17	19	0
Ordinary members *occasionally* win, even against the wishes of the leadership	16	20	21	+5*
The leadership must *quite often* change their proposals on the basis of the points of view of ordinary members	4	4	6	+2*
Difficult to say—political disagreement is rarely expressed/ Don't know, don't have enough knowledge to tell, n.a.	61	59	54	−7*
N	1890	1721	3314	

*Significant at 0.01 level.

a. Question: What is your impression of the chance of an ordinary member winning the local party branch over his/her point of view?

way most of the time. This is also not necessarily a sign of weak member influence. If it had been otherwise, the leadership, who depends on trust, probably would have been deselected at the next crossroad.

An increasing share of members considers the leadership as good at paying attention to the views of ordinary party members (figure 5.4). The proportion agreeing with this rose from 23 percent in 1991 to 37 in 2009, while between 26 and 18 percent had no

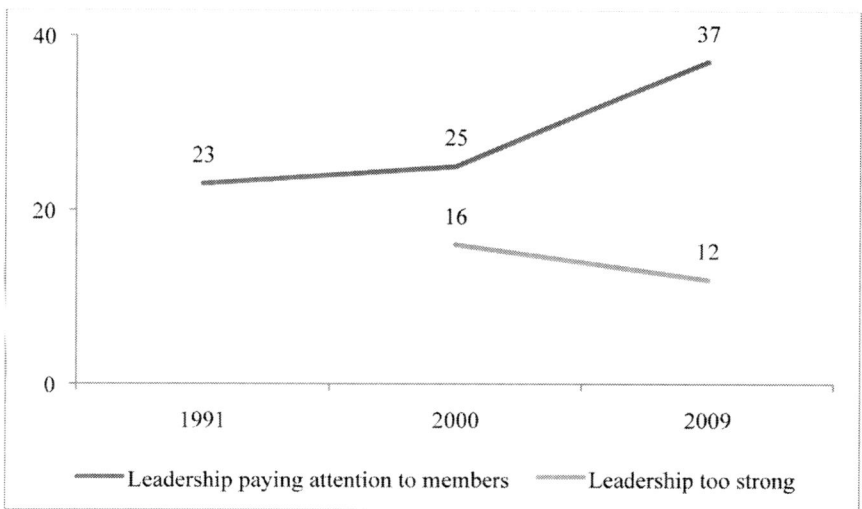

Figure 5.4. Proportion of members who agree that the leadership is paying attention to the viewpoints of ordinary members and proportion who agrees that the leadership is too strong.[7]

opinion. The majority in 1991 and 2000 answer "both and." Still it is the rising segment of the party membership that is satisfied with the leadership, and the balance of
opinion is increasingly on the side of those who think the leadership is good at listening.

In three of the parties, we find fairly high levels of those who agree that the leadership was good at paying attention (table 5A.4). In the Socialist Left (SV), Centre,
and Progress parties, the members in 2009 responded (from 45 to 57 percent) favor-
ably, while the other parties also scored high (27–34), but still on a lower level. With
the exception of the Centre and Christian parties, all had a clear rise in favorable
response from 1991 to 2009. We also see that the average increase was higher in the
no or low decline of membership parties than among the others. This is an effect of
the measurement, as both the Labour and the Conservative parties increased equally
as much as the other parties. Only the Centre and Christian parties remained basically unchanged. On this basis, we cannot claim that declining membership parties
foster a less responsive leadership.

This rather favorable view on party leadership, in support of the internal democracy experience, is brought out even more when we consider the perception of leadership strength. The members were asked if they consider it "a problem with party
today . . . that the leadership is too strong." This question was not asked in 1991,
but the 2000 survey show that 39 percent disagreed, and that the level of disagreement members had in 2009 increased to 47 percent (figure 5.4). Over 40 percent
neither agreed nor disagreed. In other words, close to half of the membership did not
consider the party leadership "too strong." Only about one in seven agreed, indicating fairly low member dissatisfaction with the party leadership. From the member
perspective, there is high and increasing satisfaction with how democracy works
inside the parties. Looking at the different parties (not shown) there are no signs that
the membership decline parties are different from the others. The Christian Party
members are somewhat more prone to agree. The Labour Party is the only major
exception to the general trend, with 14 percentage point decline. Again, to turn to
the contextual explanations, this is most likely a reflection of the turbulence emerging from an intense internal leadership debate, with strong accusations of a weak and
flawed leadership in the Labour Party around 2000.

Consequently, there *is next to nothing in the material presented above supporting the
view that party member influence on party decision-making has decreased during two
decades of massive membership decline.* If anything, we may conclude that internal
party democracy functions better today than it did in the early 1990s, at least as seen
from the member perspective. In their view, the member influence has actually increased over the years, rather than the contrary. We also do not find any support for
the proposition that parties with a large loss of members are less part of this general
trend than the other parties.

DISCUSSION AND CONCLUSION

In this chapter, we have discussed three empirical issues in the wake of Norwegian
parties' decline as membership organizations: Have member activities decreased? Has

the contact between the grass roots and the leadership inside the parties declined? Has members' perceived influence decreased? Our conclusion is that all questions must be answered in the negative. *Party members are active over a wide range of party arenas, and they are generally more active in 2009 than they were 20 years ago. There is also evidence for the proposition that the parties have become more open as participatory channels of communication, and that they have become more susceptible for members' influence than they used to be.*

We also asked if there are differences between the parties according to the degree of membership decline. There are many differences between the parties that are interesting from other points of view, but the overall finding is that the "high decline parties" are not much different from the rest. Most documented party differences may also be explained by particular contextual factors. In other words, if there are negative internal party effects of membership decline and increased public finance, we must look elsewhere.

The parties are, in other words, working well—or at least as well as they used to—in channeling the member views up to the party leadership. If anything, the parties have increased in participatory quality at the same time as they have declined in membership numbers. The party organizations seem to have improved as membership channels, having rid themselves disproportionately of inactive members. However, we need to qualify this conclusion. To get an indication of the overall level of party activism among the voters, we estimated the share of active party members in the citizenry as a whole for the period under examination (1991–2009). We found that at the macro level, *there are fewer active members around today to do the party work in Norwegian politics (i.e., to participate, communicate, and influence) than in the early 1990s.* Consequently, the parties, while at the same time keeping or improving their ability to channel members' policies to the party leadership, have become more restricted in reach.

In chapter 4, we saw that the two new parties in Norwegian politics—the Socialist Left and the Progress Party founded in the 1960s and 1970s, respectively—as well as the reunited, re-established Liberal Party, did not experience a membership decline similar to the old parties. In our period, they all started out at a much lower membership level. It must be added, though, that although differing from the old parties, none of these three parties have the general characteristics often attributed to the new green parties in Western Europe, with their flat structure, dual leadership, and so forth. Over time, they have also developed more in line with the mass party model (Heidar and Saglie 2002). These parties can be expected to recruit more activist members. We do not, however, find a clear trace of differences between the old and new parties in terms of activity change, only in terms of ability to keep its members.

In chapter 8, we return to these findings and discuss their theoretical implications and possible alternative explanations. The question now is whether the present activities and influence of the current membership is sufficient to maintain the representative capacity of Norwegian parties. This is the focus in subsequent chapters, starting with the social representativeness of members and activists in the party channel.

Table 5A.1. Participation at party events from 1991 to 2009. By party. Percent[a]

	SV			Ap			*Sp*			KrF			*V*			*H*			FrP		
	91	00	09	91	00	09	91	00	09	91	00	09	91	00	09	91	00	09	91	00	09
0	37	42	44	43	43	43	52	50	47	45	61	54	48	41	45	69	64	50	54	51	53
1	12	15	12	13	11	8	14	15	9	14	15	11	11	17	8	7	12	9	9	14	9
2–4	21	18	19	20	18	17	18	19	23	26	14	22	18	21	21	12	12	18	19	15	17
5+	30	25	25	24	28	32	16	16	21	15	10	13	23	21	26	12	12	23	18	20	21
N	345	295	581	281	268	428	285	227	455	286	231	440	260	277	487	213	198	458	220	225	465

a. High membership decline parties in bold.

Table 5A.2. Change in participation from 1991 to 2009. By party. Percent[a]

	SV	AP	Sp	KrF	V	H	FrP	Ap/Sp/ KrF/H	SV/V/ FrP
Internal Activities									
Discussed issues/candidates with other party members	+19	+22	+15	+6	+14	+11	+14	+13.5	+15.7
-Also addressed a party meeting or wrote for the press	+9	+12	+10	+6	+14	+10	+7	+9.5	+10
-Also took part in the preparation of motions within the party	+4	+9	+9	-1	+7	+8	-1	+6.3	+3.3
Participated in a study circle arranged by the party	-11	+1	+4	-4	-2	-4	+3	-0.8	-3.3
Member of executive committee in municipal or local party branch	—	-1	+3	-3	—	+5	+2	+1	+0.7
Held other office in municipal or local party branch	-2	+2	—	—	-1	+4	+3	+1.5	—
External Activities									
Discussed the party's policies with non-members	+3	+6	+11	+6	+7	+5	-2	+7	+2.7
Worked for the party in the last election campaign	+12	+3	+15	-4	—	+12	-6	+6.5	+2
Took part in demonstrations or other public events arranged by the party	+2	+1	+7	+1	+3	+4	-3	+3.3	+0.7
Wrote in the press, defending party policies or criticizing other parties' policies.	+2	+10	+6	+2	+4	+6	+6	+6	+4
Was member or deputy member of the municipal council	+8	+4	+12	-1	+9	+11	+15	+6.5	+10.7
Was member of a municipal committee	-1	—	+1	-3	-3	+7	+6	+1.3	+0.7
Financial Support									
Donated money to party funds or election funds (beyond membership fee)	-3	-5	-8	-5	-8	+11	—	-1.8	-3.7
N 1991/2009	345/ 581	281/ 428	285/ 455	286/ 440	260/ 487	213/ 458	220/ 465		

a. High membership decline parties in bold.

Table 5A.3. Level of politics in which members are most concerned with, change by party 1991–2009[a]

	SV	Ap	Sp	KrF	V	H	FrP	Ap/Sp/ KrF/H	SV/V/ FrP
Intern. or national politics in 2009	42	33	30	41	40	41	41	36.3	41
Change in 1991–2009	+3	+13**	+11**	+15**	+14**	+3	+3	+10.5	+6.7
Local politics in 2009	9	20	31	14	23	20	17	21.3	16.3
Change in 1991–2009	—	–4	+6	–3	+7*	+7*	+6*	+1.5	+4.3
N 1991/2009	343/ 574	274/ 424	275/ 446	265/ 431	259/ 480	209/ 452	216/ 449		

*Significant at 0.05 level.
**Significant at 0.01 level.

a. High membership decline parties in bold. Missing/n.a = not included.

Table 5A.4. The central party leadership is good at paying attention to the views of ordinary party members, change in "agree-percentage" 1991–2009[a]

	SV	Ap	Sp	KrF	V	H	FrP	Ap/Sp/ KrF/H	SV/V/ FrP
"Agree" 2009	45	31	46	34	33	27	57	34.5	45
Change 1991– 2009	+10*	+14*	–1	–1	+13*	+15*	+14*	+6.8	+12.3
N 1991/ 2009	345/ 581	281/ 428	285/ 455	286/ 440	260/ 487	213/ 458	220/ 465		

*Significant at 0.01 level.

a. High membership decline parties in bold.

NOTES

1. For some English language publications, see Heidar and Saglie 2003a; Heidar, Kosiara-Pedersen, and Saglie 2012; Allern and Saglie 2012, and Allern and Karlsen 2014a.

2. In passing we should also note that in the figure and in most tables in this chapter, we have coded missing answers as a "no" response. This is at the risk of deflating the numbers since we do not know explicitly what the right answer is for those not filling in this question. Nonetheless, the probability is high for a missing answer to reflect a "no," so excluding these respondents from the analysis probably would have unduly inflated the levels of activism.

3. Question: Have you ever contacted any of your party's representatives in public office to put forward your view on an issue or to get him/her to raise the matter officially?

Changes from 1991 to 2009 are significant at the 0.01 level.

4. Question: Have you ever contacted any of your party's representatives in public office to put forward your view on an issue or to get him/her to raise the matter officially?

The changes are significant at the 0.01 level for SV, Sp, KrF, H, and FrP, and the 0.05 level for Ap.

5. Question: Are you, generally speaking, most concerned with politics at the national level, with international politics, or is it local politics that interest you most?

Changes from 1991 to 2009 are significant at the 0.01 level for national politics and all levels.

6. This is confirmed by underlying data. More than 60 percent of the members surveyed in 2009 that were not active the last year answered "don't know" on the question on perceived influence.

7. Questions: To what extent do you agree with the following claims: 1) The central party leadership is good at paying attention to the views of ordinary party members, 2) A problem with the party today is that the leadership is too strong.

Changes 1991–2009 (paying attention) and 2000–2009 (leadership too strong) are significant at the 0.01 level.

6

Social Representation

In 1957, Henry Valen (1966) concluded that the "average nominee" for the Norwegian parliament was a man; he was between forty and sixty-five years old, and his socio-economic status was well above the level of the average voter. Have party MPs become even less representative in descriptive terms since then? If so, does this reflect increasingly unrepresentative party organizations?

In this chapter, we investigate how parties have developed as agencies for social, or more broadly, descriptive representation by examining who political parties have recruited to engage in intra-party politics and to Parliament. We concentrate on the individuals recruited into the party and to public positions. As shown in chapter 2, the call for background representation is based on the claim that a party group or assembly is seen as "representative" if it includes the same proportion of each relevant subgroup as the population from which it is elected. Many such background variables—like gender, age, education, occupation, occupational sector, class, and residence (urban/rural, center/periphery, and so on)—are discussed in the literature.[1] These are expected to carry important life experiences and interests that impact political opinions that are central to policy-making and party programs.

The key issue is whether the profiles of party members, delegates, and representatives differ compared to voters. Through party-controlled candidate selection, parties may stimulate or temper the degree of descriptive and substantive representation in the political system. Specifically, we ask if party members, delegates, and MPs have become less representative for the voters during the last two decades. We would expect this to be the case if declining membership made the party organization less able to mirror the social background of the voters. If the pool of potential party candidates changes due to the social and political profile of members, elected MPs might change as well and parties might recruit less representative politicians.

In line with the expectation that membership decline is a key factor behind such a development, we also envisage that the parties with the steepest decline in membership—Labour Party, Centre Party, Christian People's Party, and the Conservatives—had declined the most in their social congruence with voters (see chapter 3). The question, therefore, is whether fewer members (and less financial dependence on membership fees) actually mean less representative members and activists. Furthermore, what happens next when parties recruit individuals to public office? Do they present less representative or more elitist politicians for election than before?

To answer these questions, we will both compare all party members/delegates to all voters and look at individual parties and their voters. We shall concentrate on the four background variables that we can map systematically through the period and over party levels, namely, gender, education, occupation, and occupational sector. We expect general changes in the parties' representative capacity to be reflected in these background factors. However, before embarking on the empirical examination of social congruence between Norwegian voters and members, voters and delegates, and voters and MPs, we will first briefly go through the empirical studies that already exist on parties and social representation in Norway, and thereafter, describe the empirical measurements that we will use in our longitudinal analysis.

PREVIOUS RESEARCH ON SOCIAL CONGRUENCE IN NORWAY

Systematic studies of political recruitment and political elites are as old as the political science discipline itself in Norway (see Greve 1953; Valen 1954; Valen 1958; Valen 1966; Eliassen and Sælen 1971). Most of this research has concentrated on candidate selection and on elected members of Parliament (i.e., the final part of the party chain of representation).

Henry Valens' description of the typical 1957 candidate was based on a community study of the Stavanger area before the Storting elections. Later, a number of studies showed how the Parliament's composition differs from the population and the electorate at large, as far as key background variables like gender, age, education, and occupation are concerned (e.g., Hellevik 1969; Valen 1988; Matthews and Valen 1999; Narud and Valen 2000; Eliassen and Marino 2000). The MPs have been described as resembling a social elite, even if the level of education in the Storting has not been as high as in many other national assemblies (Best and Cotta 2000, 497–98; Narud and Valen 2000, 88).

Several changes over time can also be noted. Women have developed from being strongly underrepresented to enjoying good representation (but not gender balance). The average age for representatives has declined, but the middle-aged are still overrepresented compared to the youngest and oldest voters. Public employees have developed from being underrepresented to be overrepresented compared to those employed in the private sector. In terms of occupation, farmers and self-employed people have traditionally been overrepresented, but not anymore. Instead, we have witnessed a dramatically increased share of MPs whose main occupational experiences were derived from party work, not regular professions. At the same time, the level of education has risen: a large majority of the MPs have higher education today (Narud and Valen 2008). The overall development includes both increased congruence, more exclusiveness, and more changes wherein groups are over- and underrepresented. If focus is on education and occupation, however, there is good reason to ask whether "you have today a legislature of mostly career politicians," to paraphrase Matthews and Valen (1999, 136).

In this chapter, we are interested in whether changes in the composition of MPs can be linked to the preceding changes within the party membership organizations, beyond general developments in society at large like the general rise of education level, growth of public sector, and the integration of women in the labor market and public life. For example, we know that the increase of state subventions to parties has enlarged the pool of professional party candidates by allowing parties to employ more party staff at both the national and regional level. Public finance has also made party elites less dependent on membership fees and recruitment. Is the result a less socially and demographically representative membership organization as often suggested? If party members constitute the outer ring of an extended political class, a socially more skewed recruitment to Parliament will be nearly inevitable. Alternatively, is the development of membership and activist recruitment, as Scarrow and Gezgor's (2010) study might suggest, characterized by stability and diversity?

Existing Norwegian studies of members and congress delegates have focused on whether social cleavages are mirrored by the various membership and activist profiles (Heidar 1988; Heidar and Saglie 2002). They also indicate that the social profile of members and activists has changed somewhat compared to the electorate. On the one hand, party members and activists have become more socially exclusive, for example, in terms of education level. On the other hand, the share of women has increased, if not significantly, between 1989 and 2000. Men continued to be overrepresented, but not strongly, and less so among delegates than among ordinary members. In addition, party members and delegates seem overall to have become somewhat older than before (Heidar and Saglie 2002, 100–101). Finally, Putnam's (1976) Law of Increasing Disproportion seems to apply to social status variables: the propensity for party members to come from a more exclusive background rises as one moves from ordinary party members to congress delegates. However, there are also examples suggesting that congress delegates are more representative for voters than the members, for example, in terms of gender (Putnam 1976, 107).

There are indications of changing patterns of recruitment in recent decades throughout the party chain, but more detailed and systematic analysis is needed to find out whether or not this supports the proposition of declining representativeness. Few have studied the level of social congruence directly in Norway, and nobody has so far studied the development of social representation over time by looking at all the party strata together. In what follows, we compare the demography and social background of voters to party members, congress delegates, and MPs, as systematically as we can from 1989 to 2009.

MEASURING SOCIAL CONGRUENCE

As noted, we look at two demographical variables, gender and age, and three social status/background variables: level of education, occupation, and occupation sector. These are all conventional indicators that will tell us as to what extent the party affiliates resemble the electorate demographically and socially over time. The question is how to calculate a valid measure of social congruence based on such variables.

Social representativeness is often studied by *differences in percentages or difference in central tendencies* (see, e.g., Scarrow and Gezgor 2010). These measures are simple, adequate descriptions, and will be used in the following. The less difference between the various groups (voters, members, delegates, and MPs) the stronger congruence, and conversely, the larger difference, the less congruence. The expectation would be that these differences have increased over time as the party organizations declined. Whether these differences are positive or negative does not matter for the level of representative capacity as it is the numeric size that indicates the degree of congruence. The positive/negative sign will only tell which groups are over- or underrepresented.

However, when looking at nominal or ordinal variables with more than two (but not many) values, like in the case of education levels or occupation groups, we need an alternative and suggest using Gallagher's index of disproportionality (least square index).[2] This was created to measure the disproportionality of an electoral outcome: that is, the difference between the percentage of votes received and the percentage of seats a party gets in parliament. Yet it can also be used to measure the difference between the distributions of two groups. The index takes the square root of half the sum of the squares of the difference between the group percentages, and differs between zero (perfect congruence) and 100 (no congruence):

$$\text{LSq} = \sqrt{\frac{1}{2} \sum_{i=1}^{n} (V_i - S_i)^2}$$

in which V stands for the voters and S for the seats or, in this context, members/delegates/MPs. To decide what is high and what is low social congruence based on GDI scores is not straightforward. As will be further discussed in this chapter regarding policy congruence, everything close to perfect congruence is to be considered a truly high level of congruence. A GDI score of around 10 will be characterized as a very low level of disproportionality and close to perfect social congruence. Somewhat higher but still fairly low scores (above 10) will be considered as limited disproportionality and a fairly high level of congruence. The closer we get to 100, the stronger the degree of disproportionality and the weaker the degree of congruence.

DATA MATERIAL

Our data consist of surveys of voters, members, and delegates, and of MP biographies for three different points in time: around 1990, 2000, and around 2010 (see table 6.1). The data on MPs were collected by the Parliament and coded by Narud and her assistants. The surveys were not conducted as a joint research project. The questions and categories used are very similar, but not always identical. We will highlight such differences in due course. As a consequence, we must be careful with the interpretations. Even when similar questions had been asked, different categorization methods may affect congruence patterns. Therefore, only major variations should be emphasized. To enable comparison with voter surveys, respondents in the party member surveys who are *not* between 18 and 79 years old have been excluded from the analyses. As the delegate survey includes the entire population and are not sampled, we have generally kept all respondents here. Very few delegates are younger or older than 18/79 (less than five in sum of both years), but these were nonetheless excluded when analyzing age disparity. In the MP biographies, the problem was non-existent as all MPs are at least 18 years old, and no one was older than 79 between 1989 and 2009.[3]

Table 6.1. Data used in the chapter

	Voters	*Members*	*Delegates*	*MPs*
1990	NES 1989	Member survey 1991	Non-existent	MP Biographies 1989
2000	NES 2001	Member survey 2000	Delegate survey 2001	MP Biographies 2001
2010	NES 2009	Member survey 2009	Delegate survey 2009	MP Biographies 2009

EMPIRICAL ANALYSIS

In what follows, we study whether Norwegian party members, delegates, and MPs mirror the electorate in terms of demography and social background. The empirical analysis is organized variable by variable, starting with gender and age. For each variable, we first present the general development across parties. Then, we look at possible party differences.

Gender

Previous studies of participation in political parties and recruitment to parliament have consistently found party membership and parliaments to be disproportionally male. However, this has decreased somewhat in Norway. Figure 6.1 reveals that men are still overrepresented in the party chain—from ordinary members to MPs—but nearly 40 percent of the party membership is female, and gender congruence has not changed much since 1989 at any level. To the extent that changes can be identified, they are toward *increased* gender proportionality. The delegate level is more balanced than both the membership level and the MPs. Hence, even if women are better represented at the party congress than among the party grass roots, the candidate selection does not provide the same overall selection result (despite the use of gender quotas in some parties).

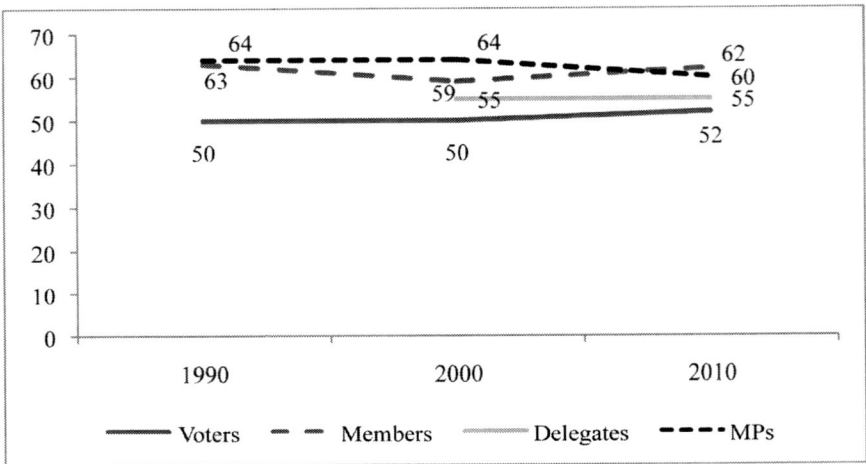

Figure 6.1. Gender congruence 1989–2009: the proportion of men amongst voters, party members (M), delegates (D), and MPs.

Table 6.2 presents gender congruence by party to measure to what extent individual parties mirror the distribution of gender among their voters. We see that there are differences between parties in terms of gender proportionality at all levels, and that individual parties fluctuate across the levels and over time.

To illustrate, SV's gender congruence was perfect in 1989 at the membership level, but it increased to nearly 10 percent by overrepresentation of male voters in 2009. Radical changes are found in the Centre Party (Sp), where women have clearly become better represented at all levels over time. Today, male voters are underrepresented among Centre Party delegates and MPs. This change reflects more female MPs, but also that the Sp electorate has become dominated by men (about 60 percent men in 2009). The huge gender change in the Liberal's (V) parliamentary group is most likely largely due to size. In 2009, this party only included two MPs, who were both women. In Progress (FrP), the party with most male voters—more than 60 percent at all times—the overrepresentation of men has gradually decreased at all levels. Most importantly, we see that there is no *general* trend toward *decreased* gender congruence across party strata and parties. We do not find that the parties that have lost most members since the 1980s—Ap, Sp, KrF, and Høyre (H)—have experienced a systematic, steep decrease in congruence. Taken together, parties represent the electorate fairly well in terms of gender today, especially at the party congresses.

Table 6.2. Gender congruence 1989–2009 by party: difference in percentage male party voters (V) compared to party members (M), delegates (D), and MPs[a]

	1990				2000[b]				2010			
	V % Male	V-M	V-D	V-MP	V % Male	V-M	V-D	V-MP	V % Male	V-M	V-D	V-MP
SV	43	0	n.a.	+16	40	+3	+11	+12	38	+9	+12	+35
Ap	49	+14	n.a.	0	47	+13	+3	+7	48	+12	+3	+2
Sp	49	+22	n.a.	+24	52	+20	+3	+12	61	+7	+8	+25
KrF	44	+4	n.a.	+20	39	+5	+17	+25	46	+3	+4	+14
V[c]	59	+1	n.a.	n.a.	57	+4	+2	+43	44	+18	+13	+44
H	51	+18	n.a.	+19	56	+7	+4	+10	54	+13	+4	+16
FrP	63	+11	n.a.	+33	64	+9	+14	+25	66	+8	+5	+10

a. For the N's, see Table 4.5.
b. Labour Party delegate survey is from 2000.
c. The Liberal Party (V) did not have MPs from 1989–1993, and only two from 2001–2005 and 2009–2013.

Age

In Western Europe, the average age of party members has traditionally been higher than the average age of the population.[4] Age structure seems more likely to be affected by the decline of membership figures than gender representation, as, to paraphrase Scarrow and Gezgor (2010, 830), "in many parties, the drop in membership apparently has affected the enrolment of new (younger) members more steeply than the retention of existing (older) members."

From figure 6.2, we see that the average party member is older than the average voter at all three points in time, but not increasingly so. Age congruence is generally

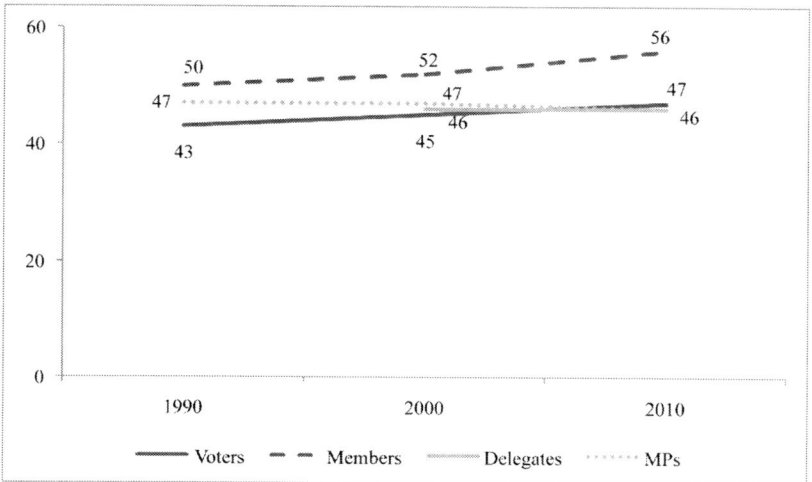

Figure 6.2. Age congruence 1989–2009: average age of voters (V) compared to party members (M), delegates (D), and MPs.[5]

better at the delegate level and among MPs than at the level of members. In 2009, it seems as if both delegates and MPs are, on average, slightly *younger* than the average voter. Norwegian parties do not tend to recruit older politicians: the average age of MPs has decreased slightly and the average age today is about 46 years (Allern, Karlsen, and Narud 2014).

Another way of measuring age disparities is to compare the proportion of the general electorate belonging to different age groups with similar figures for the various party strata. In table 6.3, we have divided the voters into three categories: those between 18 and 30, 31 and 50, and those over 50 (but under 80, see above). The point here is not primarily the age groups as such, but to get a more differentiated measurement. To measure the overall congruence for each level, we use Gallagher's disproportionality index.

Table 6.3. Age congruence 1989–2009: percentage shares of different age groups and Gallagher's disproportionality index (GDI): voters (V) compared to party members (M), delegates (D), and MPs[a]

	1990				2000				2010			
	18–30	31–50	51+	GDI	18–30	31–50	51+	GDI	18–30	31–50	51+	GDI
Voters	28	39	33		22	41	38		18	39	43	
(V-) M[b]	12	39	49	16	11	32	58	17.4	6	28	66	19.9
(V-) D[c]	n.a.	n.a.	n.a.	n.a.	16	42	42	5.2	16	43	40	3.8
(V-) MP	8	59	33	20	9	47	44	11	7	55	39	14

a. Member and delegate figures have been weighted by the number of party members in each party to take into account variation in party size (see the discussion in chapter 4). For the N's, see table 4.5.
b. Member survey is from 1991.
c. There was no delegate survey in 1989.

First, we conclude that the level of disproportionality is (fairly) low (20 or below). Age congruence appears to be good at all levels and over time. There is no *general* tendency toward increasing age disparities. However, following the increase of the average member's age (figure 6.2), we see that the GDI score for voter-members is marginally higher in 2009 than in 1989. The oldest group is clearly overrepresented among party members, and this disparity is stable, or has increased slightly since 1989. The middle aged (31–50) seems to be overrepresented at all party levels, most strongly among MPs, but not increasingly so. Most importantly, the tendency toward increased age disproportionality at the membership level of parties has *not* led to worse age congruence between voters and congress delegates and MPs as defined here.

Table 6.4 presents the age congruence by party. The level of disproportionality seems low (below 20) across parties and time, though with a few exceptions. One party has generally improved its age representativeness (H), while another displays weaker general congruence since 1989 across levels (KrF). However, to the extent that changes have occurred, most parties seem to have developed in different ways at different levels. There is no general tendency toward increasing age disparities. Not all the parties' members have become less representative in terms of age: the GDI score seems stable in the Conservative (H), Progress (FrP), and the Liberal Parties (V).

Table 6.4.   Age congruence 1989–2009 by party, Gallagher's disproportionality index (GDI): party voters (V) compared to party members (M), delegates (D), and MPs[a]

	1990			2000			2010		
	V-M[b]	V-D[c]	V-MP	V-M	V-D	V-MP	V-M	V-D	V-MP
SV	8.5	n.a.	23.6	14	7.3	6.8	16.5	9	8.6
Ap	10.8	n.a.	14.9	15.6	1.7	7.9	17.8	9.2	12.1
Sp	11	n.a.	16.9	11.3	10.5	11.1	23.5	1.6	20.7
KrF	6.9	n.a.	29.6	8.5	1.7	16.2	18.3	5.6	33.7
V	10.7	n.a.	n.a.	12.7	9.7	13.9	8.5	10.2	4.7
H	23.3	n.a.	25.9	21.2	4.6	8.7	21.9	6.6	10.4
FrP	10	n.a.	19.5	11.1	17.5	18.9	11.8	17.7	19.9

a. For the age categories on which the calculations are made, see table 6.3. For percentage shares, see table 6A.1.
b. Member survey is from 1991.
c. There was no delegate survey in 1989.

Education

In most advanced democracies, people with higher education have been over-represented in both party organizations and parliamentary groups. General over-representation is still the case in Norway (see table 6.5 and figure 6.3), even though different wording of survey questions calls for careful interpretation of the results. The propensity for party affiliates to have university education rises as one moves from ordinary party members to congress delegates to MPs. Putnam's "Law of Increasing Disproportion" seems to apply. At the membership level, the congruence is good (GDI score around 10).

Table 6.5.   Education congruence 1989–2009: percentage shares of different educational levels[a]: voters (V) compared to party members (M), delegates (D), and MPs[b]

	1990			2000			2010		
	Low	Medium	High	Low	Medium	High	Low	Medium	High
Voters	24	57	19	16	59	25	14	45	41
Members[c]	33	45	22	23	44	33	15	37	49
Delegates[d]	n.a.	n.a.	n.a.	9	35	56	4	25	70
MPs	1	39	60	2	24	75	2	21	76

a. "Low" = compulsory primary and lower secondary school, "medium" = upper secondary school, "high" = university college or university (started or completed degree).
b. Member survey is from 1991.
c. Member and delegate figures have been weighted by the number of party members in each party to take into account variation in party size (see the discussion in chapter 4). For unweighted N's, see appendix.
d. There was no delegate survey in 1989.

The overall congruence appears to have weakened from 1989 to 2001, but it strengthened again in 2001 and 2009 at all levels. The latter development could be due to a methodological factor: about 40 percent of the voters report to have higher education in 2009, compared to 25 in 2001. According to Statistics Norway, the share of citizens (above 16) who had a higher education in 1990 was 16 percent. In 2001, it was 23 percent. In 2009, it increased to 28 percent.[6] There seems to be a significant degree of over-reporting in 2009, which is probably related to the fact that on this year, the coding in the election studies was based on survey responses and not on public records, as in previous years. With only about 28 percent of the voters having higher education in 2009, the percentage difference of V-MP seems fairly stable, and the share of delegates with higher education increased from about 55 to about 70 percent, thereby approaching the MP level.[7] Hence, we may conclude that as far as education is concerned, the representation of voters has become less proportional since the 1990s throughout the party chain, and not least among the congress delegates and MPs, even if the latter disparity may have leveled out or decreased a bit after 2001.

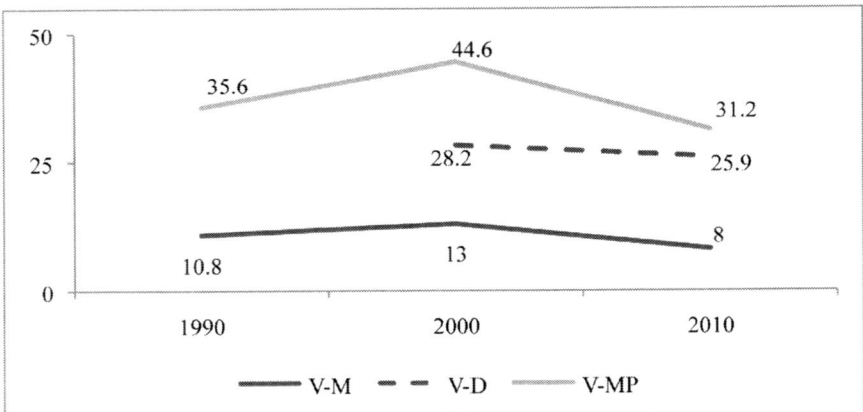

Figure 6.3.   Education congruence 1989–2009: Gallagher's disproportionality index (GDI): voters (V) compared to party members (M), delegates (D), and MPs.

Table 6.6 presents the education level congruence by party with each party's electorate as reference category. The over-reporting of higher education in 2009 is a challenge, as it is difficult to say whether consistent differences exist between parties over time when it comes to the development of voter-MP education congruence. Nevertheless, we see that all parties obtain a score above 25 at all points in time at the MP level, and three above 50 in 2001 (SV, KrF, and H). Most parties' GDI score for voters and MPs increases from 1989 to 2001. Nonetheless, Labour has become *more* representative for their voters since 1989, seemingly because the share of social democratic voters with higher education has grown (see table 6A.2 in the appendix). Finally, parties seem generally more representative for their voters at the membership level than at the two other levels. Again it is difficult to say whether consistent differences exist between parties over time.

Table 6.6. Education congruence 1989–2009 by party, Gallagher's disproportionality index: party voters (V) compared to party members (M), delegates (D), and MPs[a]

	1990			2000			2010		
	V-M[b]	V-D[c]	V-MP	V-M	V-D	V-MP	V-M	V-D	V-MP
SV	21.7	n.a.	39.5	29.7	29	53.6	14.7	13.5	32.4
Ap	13.1	n.a.	39.2	18.5	21	27.7	9.1	24.9	25.1
Sp	17.8	n.a.	41.3	11.1	36.1	48	5.3	25.7	53.7
KrF	13.1	n.a.	29.1	21.1	38.7	60.5	1.7	21.7	33.9
V	15.1	n.a.	n.a.	6.4	16.8	40.3	14.5	26.2	35.8
H	6	n.a.	38.4	13.1	31	52.1	1.6	16.5	29.2
FrP	11.3	n.a.	37.4	3.2	16.7	37.7	5.8	28.3	34.9

a. For the education levels on which the calculations are made, see table 6.5. For percentage shares, see appendix.
b. Member survey is from 1991.
c. There was no delegate survey in 1989.

Occupation

Occupation is a key variable when trying to measure social background. Traditionally, white-collar employees have been overrepresented in the party sphere. However, as in the case of education levels, the categorization of the different occupations is not straightforward. While voters (2001 and 2009) and MPs have mentioned their specific occupation and position, members, delegates, and 1989 voters have placed themselves in predefined, broad categories. In addition, while the voters in 2001 and 2009 were categorized based on the International Standard Classification of Occupations (ISCO), MPs have been coded by the research group in line with previous Norwegian (and comparative) studies of representation. Therefore, the figures are not directly comparable across surveys. The specific categories used are defined in the table note (table 6.7), including other sources of subsistence other than employed work.[8]

First, we may note that the level of disproportionality seems low overall at the membership and delegate level (GDI score below 20 on average [see figure 6.4]), but that the disproportionality is a bit stronger when we move to the MPs (GDI score around 30). Consequently, Putnam's law might apply.

Second, and most important here, the changes over time since 1989 seem to be generally limited, and they do not follow a uniform pattern across levels. It seems as if primary industry voters and self-employed voters are well represented throughout the period, and that farmers and fishermen are decreasingly overrepresented. The most notable change seems to have occurred among higher white-collar employees, who are increasingly overrepresented at the higher party levels, even if it should be noted that the voter survey applies a more limited definition of senior (high) positions than the other sources. In 2009, 25 percent of the congress delegates and 50 percent of the MPs had such a background compared to 9 percent of voters and 12 percent of the party members. Pensioners are clearly underrepresented at both the delegate and MP level throughout the period.

Table 6.7.   Occupation congruence 1989–2009: percentage shares of different occupation categories[a][b]

	Worker	White-collar, low	White-collar, medium	White-collar, high	Primary industry	Self employed	Student	Pensioner	Homemaker
				1990					
Voters	18	15	14	10	4	7	6	20	7
M[c]	12	10	13	14	8	10	7	24	3
D[d]	n.a.	n.a.	n.a.	n.a.	n.a	n.a.	n.a.	n.a.	n.a.
MPs	2	6	26	44	9	8	2	1	3
				2000					
Voters	12	14	24	7	2	5	9	23	4
M	13	4	18	12	7	8	6	28	3
D	7	5	24	27	4	11	14	7	1
MPs	5	6	29	42	4	6	7	0	1
				2010					
Voters	10	13	29	9	2	5	9	23	1
M	13	4	20	12	4	10	3	34	1
D	12	6	24	25	3	9	12	9	1
MPs	5	5	21	50	4	6	8	0	1

a. Occupation (or source of subsistence): Worker = ordinary and trained worker, craftsman, and so on; White-collar low = subordinated level (shop assistants, clerks, and so on); White-collar medium = mid-level (teacher, nurse, engineer, and so on); White-collar high = superior/chief position at mid- or top-level in public or private unit; Primary industry (farmers, fishermen, and so on); Self-employed (company owners, independent professionals like dentists, lawyers, and so on); Pensioners; Students; Homemakers.
b. Member and delegate figures have been weighted by the number of party members in each party to take into account variation in party size (see the discussion in chapter 4). For unweighted N's, see appendix.
c. Member survey is from 1991.
d. There was no delegate survey in 1989.

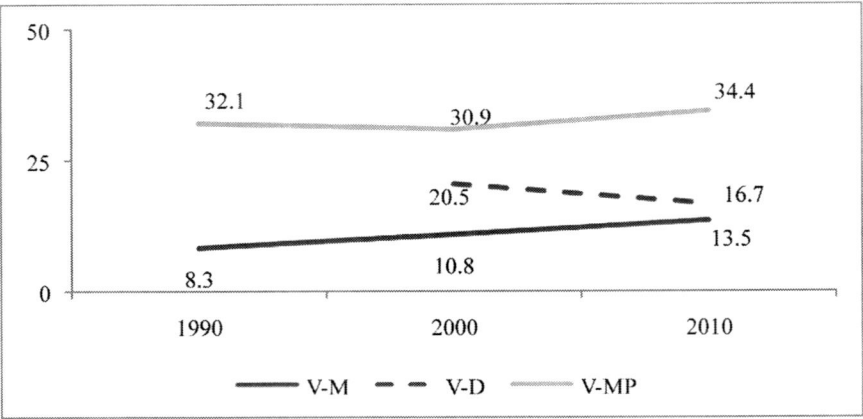

Figure 6.4.   Occupation congruence: Gallagher's disproportionality index (GDI): voters (V) compared to party members (M), delegates (D), and MPs.

The analyses on the individual parties reveal the same tendency (table 6.8). Members resemble the voters most, and MPs resemble voters the least. There is also a slight tendency toward members and MPs to become less representative for voters over time. Still, members resemble voters to a much greater extent than MPs. As for the individual parties, no party stands out as the one that represents the voters best for all years. The GDI for voters and members is particularly low for Ap, KrF, and V in 1990, but in 2010, members in the Liberal and Progress parties resemble the voters most.

Table 6.8. Occupation congruence 1989–2009 by party, Gallagher's disproportionality index: party voters (V) compared to party members (M), delegates (D), and MPs[a]

	1990			*2000*			*2010*		
	V-M[b]	*V-D*[c]	*V-MP*	*V-M*	*V-D*	*V-MP*	*V-M*	*V-D*	*V-MP*
SV	23.6	n.a.	39.6	16.4	19.5	43.2	20.5	22.3	63.7
Ap	11.1	n.a.	52.1	21.7	28.5	41.4	27.1	26.7	58.4
Sp	18.7	n.a.	45.4	16.6	33.7	51.7	23.9	29.0	38.2
KrF	10.6	n.a.	46.3	15.8	34.4	55.2	29.3	26.4	79.8
V	9.8	n.a.	37.8	24.8	28.5	79.0	15.9	24.8	49.1
H	18.2	n.a.	44.0	22.8	17.3	43.5	31.0	20.0	37.9
FrP	19.6	n.a.	58.3	22.9	38.3	51.7	16.1	29.4	46.3
Mean	15.9	n.a.	47.6	20.1	28.6	47.8	23.4	25.5	54.1

a. For the occupation/subsistence categories on which the calculations are made, see table 6.7. For percentage shares, see table 6A.3.
b. Member survey is from 1991.
c. There was no delegate survey in 1989.

Sector

Sector is the final social background variable to be considered. In figure 6.5, we see that the level of disproportionality seems low overall at the membership and delegate level (GDI score below 20 on average), but that the disproportionality is slightly stronger when we move up to the MPs. On the whole, limited changes have occurred over time at the delegate and membership level. To the extent that the differences actually exist, the development indicates slightly enhanced representation in 2009 compared to previous years. At the MP level, in contrast, the disproportionality score has increased from around 15 in 1990 to 24 in 2009. From previous studies of Norwegian MPs, we know that public employees have developed from being underrepresented to being overrepresented compared to those employed in the private sector. We see from table 6.9 that in 2001, the private sector was underrepresented at all levels of the party, and increasingly so as we move toward the Parliament. Public employees, as well as those employed in the associational life, have also become overrepresented. Indeed, in 2009 there was near parity in Parliament for the public group, whereas employees *in organizations* were clearly overrepresented. This development probably reflects the steep increase of MPs with their main occupational experience deriving from party work in recent years (Narud and Valen 2008).

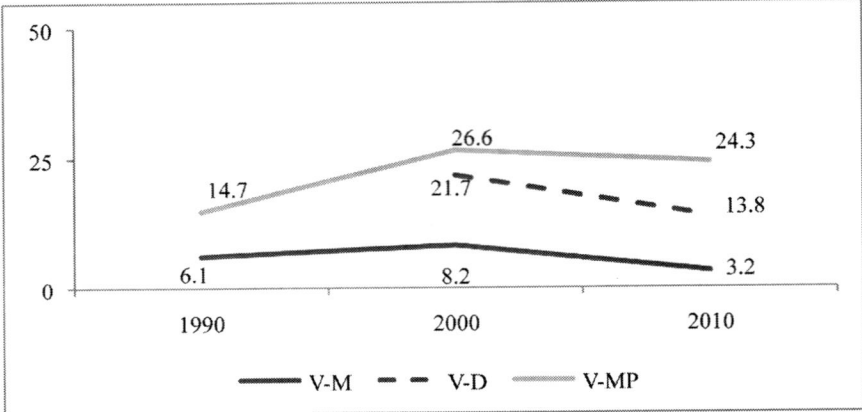

Figure 6.5. Sector congruence 1989–2009: Gallagher's disproportionality index (GDI): voters (V) compared to party members (M), delegates (D), and MPs.

Table 6.9. Sector congruence 1989–2009: percentage shares of different sector affiliations[a]: voters (V) compared to party members (M), delegates (D), and MPs[b]

	1990			2000			2010		
	Private	Public	Org.	Private	Public	Org.	Private	Public	Org.
Voters	53	44	4	59	38	4	53	44	3
M[c]	58	37	5	50	45	6	52	42	7
D[d]	n.a.	n.a.	n.a.	34	50	17	38	47	15
MPs	37	47	17	29	49	21	31	40	29

a. Employees in the private sector, public sector, and in various organizations. Pensioners, students, and housewives are excluded.
b. Member and delegate figures have been weighted by the number of party members in each party to take into account variation in party size (see the discussion in chapter 4). For unweighted N's, see appendix.
c. Member survey is from 1991.
d. There was no delegate survey in 1989.

Finally, when looking at individual parties (see table 6.10), we may note that the level of sector disproportionality is generally low at the membership level (below 20, and very low in some cases), with the exception of Sp in 2009 (30). We also see that in many parties, disproportionality is generally stronger at the MP level than at lower levels. In all parties, the disproportionality score for voters and MPs increased between 1989 and 2001/2009. Similarly, there were differences between parties and over time, but there was no clear pattern.

Table 6.10. Sector congruence in 1989–2009 by party, Gallagher's disproportionality index: party voters (V) compared to party members (M), delegates (D), and MPs[a]

	1990			2000			2010		
	V-M[b]	*V-D*[c]	*V-MP*	*V-M*	*V-D*	*V-MP*	*V-M*	*V-D*	*V-MP*
SV	10.8	n.a.	16.5	17.1	18.3	13.1	1.6	10	23.4
Ap	2.7	n.a.	22.1	6.9	21.8	17.6	6.2	13.8	27.8
Sp	18.7	n.a.	5.6	3	21.3	14.1	30.1	15.7	27.5
KrF	4.2	n.a.	20.3	19.7	27.6	46.1	5.5	11	25.5
V	12.1	n.a.	n.a.	3.8	7.1	38.4	11.1	10.4	37.4
H	14.5	n.a.	15.6	4.5	19.1	41.1	1.6	9.7	25.3
FrP	3.5	n.a.	26.7	2.6	7.2	18.6	3.2	13.7	32.6

a. For the sector categories on which the calculations are made, see table 6.9. For percentage shares, see table 6A.4.
b. Member survey is from 1991.
c. There was no delegate survey in 1989.

DISCUSSION AND CONCLUSION

The results in this chapter do not indicate a *general* decline in social congruence across party levels and between parties. However, when it comes to descriptive representation, the parties' representative capacity has not been stable since 1989. Let us briefly summarize our main and mixed findings.

Men—from ordinary members to MPs—are still overrepresented in the Norwegian party chain, but not strongly. To the extent that changes can be identified overall, they are toward increased gender proportionality. We conclude that there is no general trend toward declining gender congruence across parties. The average party member is older than the average voter at all three points in time, but not increasingly so. In 2009, both delegates and MPs are, on average, younger than the average voter. In terms of age groups, age congruence appears to be good at all levels and over time, even if the middle aged seems to be overrepresented at all party levels, and most strongly among MPs. The oldest group is clearly overrepresented among party members at present; this disparity has increased since 1989. This age increase is the clearest change in the social composition of party membership in the last 20 years. This change, however, has not made the average MP older.

As far as education is concerned, the representation of voters has become less proportional since 1989 throughout the party chain, and not least among congress delegates and MPs. This tendency is also notable in most parties individually. With regard to occupation congruence, the level of disproportionality seems low overall. Changes since 1990 appear limited and do not follow a uniform pattern across levels. The most notable change seems to have occurred in the representation of higher white-collar employees; this group is increasingly overrepresented at the higher party levels. Pensioners are clearly underrepresented at both the delegate and MP levels throughout the period.

As far as sector representation is concerned, limited changes have occurred over time at the delegate and membership level. At the MP level, however, the disproportionality score increased. Public employees, as well as those employed in the associational life, have become overrepresented. In 2009, employees in organizations are clearly overrepresented. Probably, this development reflects the steep increase of MPs in recent years, with their main occupational experiences derived from party work. The analyses of individual parties present a more complex picture. There is no clear pattern of cross-party variation. There are, for example, differences between parties in terms of sector representation, but the differences vary over time. Hence, this study does not find that the parties that have lost most members since the 1980s (Ap, Sp, KrF, and Høyre [H]) have experienced a systematic decrease of demographic and social congruence. Moreover, the fact that the total number of MPs is very small in some parties makes some results difficult to interpret.

To conclude, *there is no clear general trend toward weakened congruence across party levels*. This way, the study echoes Scarrow and Gezgor's (2010, 836) findings on stable social congruence as far as European party members go. Our results suggest that Norwegian party (membership) organizations have *not* become "the outer ring of an extended political class" despite significant membership decline. That said, we have revealed that the party members have become less representative for voters in terms of age (older), and to some extent, education. Members of parliament are less similar to voters than they used to be in terms of education, occupation, and sector affiliation. Those with higher education, those working as senior white collar employees, and those employed in the public sector or by organizations (parties) have all become more strongly overrepresented in Parliament.

In chapter 8, we will scrutinize these findings further after examining the other main aspects of representation, as well as the development of policy congruence between voters, members, delegates, and MPs, during the same time period.

APPENDIX

Table 6A.1. Age congruence in 1989–2009 by party: percentage shares of different age groups and Gallagher's disproportionality index (GDI): party voters (V) compared to party members (M), delegates (D), and MPs

SV	1990				2000				2010			
	−30	*31–50*	*51+*	*GDI*	*−30*	*31–50*	*51+*	*GDI*	*−30*	*31–50*	*51+*	*GDI*
Voters	36	48	16		28	47	25		18	44	38	
(V-) Mª	28	57	15	8.5	14	61	25	14	10	33	57	16.5
(V-) Dᵇ	n.a.	n.a.	n.a.	n.a.	20	53	28	7.3	23	34	44	9
(V-) MP	12	71	18	23.6	30	52	17	6.8	9	46	46	8.6

Ap	1990				2000				2010			
	−30	*31–50*	*51+*	*GDI*	*−30*	*31–50*	*51+*	*GDI*	*−30*	*31–50*	*51+*	*GDI*
Voters	19	42	39		11	41	48		14	39	47	
(V-) M	14	34	51	10.8	13	25	63	15.6	8	25	67	17.8
(V-) D	n.a.	n.a.	n.a.	n.a	12	42	46	1.7	16	47	37	9.2
(V-) MP	8	59	33	14.9	2	44	54	7.9	13	52	36	12.1

Sp	1990				2000				2010			
	−30	*31–50*	*51+*	*GDI*	*−30*	*31–50*	*51+*	*GDI*	*−30*	*31–50*	*51+*	*GDI*
Voters	19	38	43		10	42	48		17	41	42	
(V-) M	8	38	54	11	4	35	61	11.3	6	25	69	23.5
(V-) D	n.a.	n.a.	n.a.	n.a.	21	41	38	10.5	15	41	43	1.6
(V-) MP	0	46	55	16.9	0	40	60	11.1	0	64	36	20.7

KrF	1990				2000				2010			
	−30	*31–50*	*51+*	*GDI*	*−30*	*31–50*	*51+*	*GDI*	*−30*	*31–50*	*51+*	*GDI*
Voters	14	30	56		13	42	45		22	22	56	
(V-) M	6	34	60	6.9	12	34	54	8.5	2	26	72	18.3
(V-) D	n.a.	n.a.	n.a.	n.a.	12	41	47	1.7	16	27	57	5.6
(V-) MP	0	64	36	29.6	5	32	64	16.2	10	60	30	33.7

V	1990				2000				2010			
	−30	*31–50*	*51+*	*GDI*	*−30*	*31–50*	*51+*	*GDI*	*−30*	*31–50*	*51+*	*GDI*
Voters	32	45	23		16	41	43		17	41	42	
(V-) M	23	43	35	10.7	9	34	58	12.7	9	40	51	8.5
(V-) D	n.a.	n.a.	n.a.	n.a.	18	49	32	9.7	28	39	33	10.2
(V-) MPᶜ	n.a	n.a.	n.a	n.a.	0	50	50	13.9	0	50	50	14.7

(continued)

Table 6A.1. *Continued*

H	1990 -30	31–50	51+	GDI	2000 -30	31–50	51+	GDI	2010 -30	31–50	51+	GDI
Voters	31	39	30		17	45	38		12	46	42	
(V-) M	6	43	51	23.3	9	29	62	21.2	3	30	67	21.9
(V-) D	n.a.	n.a.	n.a.	n.a.	21	40	39	4.6	18	39	43	6.6
(V-) MP	3	62	35	25.9	11	55	34	8.7	0	53	47	10.4

FrP	1990 -30	31–50	51+	GDI	2000 -30	31–50	51+	GDI	2010 -30	31–50	51+	GDI
Voters	42	30	28		16	32	52		14	38	48	
(V-) M	46	38	17	10	14	44	42	11.1	7	32	62	11.8
(V-) D	n.a.	n.a.	n.a.	n.a.	15	50	35	17.5	11	57	32	17.7
(V-) MP	23	50	27	19.5	8	54	39	18.9	2	61	37	19.9

a. Member survey is from 1991.
b. There was no delegate survey in 1989.
c. The Liberal Party was not represented in Parliament from 1989–1993, and only had two MPs in the periods 2001–2005 and 2009–2013.

Table 6A.2. Education congruence in 1989–2009 by party: percentage shares of different educational levels[a] and Gallagher's disproportionality index (GDI): party voters (V) compared to party members (M), delegates (D), and MPs[b]

SV	1990				2000				2010			
	High	Med.	Low	GDI	High	Med.	Low	GDI	High	Med.	Low	GDI
Voters	14	54	32		9	52	38		6	29	65	
(V-) M	11	34	55	21.7	5	25	70	29.7	3	16	81	14.7
(V-) D[c]	n.a.	n.a.	n.a.	n.a.	3	27	70	29	2	18	80	13.5
(V-) MP	0	24	77	39.5	0	4	96	53.6	0	0	100	32.4

Ap	1990				2000				2010			
	High	Med.	Low	GDI	High	Med.	Low	GDI	High	Med.	Low	GDI
Voters	37	55	8		18	58	24		18	42	40	
(V-) M	49	41	9	13.1	37	40	23	18.5	22	32	47	9.1
(V-) D[c]	n.a.	n.a.	n.a.	n.a.	13	40	47	21	6	26	69	24.9
(V-) MP	0	51	49	39.2	2	42	56	27.7	3	28	69	25.1

Sp	1990				2000				2010			
	High	Med.	Low	GDI	High	Med.	Low	GDI	High	Med.	Low	GDI
Voters	25	68	7		16	68	16		10	48	42	
(V-) M	41	49	11	17.8	26	56	18	11.1	14	50	36	5.3
(V-) D[c]	n.a.	n.a.	n.a.	n.a.	4	40	57	36.1	3	26	70	25.7
(V-) MP	0	46	55	41.3	0	30	70	48	0	0	100	53.7

KrF	1990				2000				2010			
	High	Med.	Low	GDI	High	Med.	Low	GDI	High	Med.	Low	GDI
Voters	25	50	25		15	60	24		11	37	52	
(V-) M	40	40	21	13.1	21	37	42	21.1	13	36	51	1.7
(V-) D[c]	n.a.	n.a.	n.a.	n.a.	4	28	67	38.7	3	21	77	21.7
(V-) MP	0	43	57	29.1	0	9	91	60.5	0	10	90	33.9

V	1990				2000				2010			
	High	Med.	Low	GDI	High	Med.	Low	GDI	High	Med.	Low	GDI
Voters	10	53	37		6	37	57		5	33	62	
(V-) M	15	36	49	15.1	9	30	62	6.4	4	19	77	14.5
(V-) D[c]	n.a.	n.a.	n.a.	n.a.	0	24	76	16.8	1	9	90	26.2
(V-) MP[d]	n.a.	n.a.	n.a.	n.a.	0	0	100	40.3	0	0	100	35.8

(continued)

Table 6A.2.   *Continued*

H	1990				2000				2010			
	High	Med.	Low	GDI	High	Med.	Low	GDI	High	Med.	Low	GDI
Voters	12	55	33		9	60	31		4	37	59	
(V-) M	18	49	34	6	11	46	43	13.1	4	35	60	1.6
(V-) D[c]	n.a.	n.a.	n.a.	n.a.	9	29	62	31	3	21	76	16.5
(V-) MP	0	24	76	38.4	0	13	87	52.1	0	10	90	29.2

FrP	1990				2000				2010			
	High	Med.	Low	GDI	High	Med.	Low	GDI	High	Med.	Low	GDI
Voters	20	68	12		26	59	14		21	58	21	
(V-) M	27	55	18	11.3	24	59	18	3.2	18	55	28	5.8
(V-) D[c]	n.a.	n.a.	n.a.	n.a.	13	54	33	16.7	5	42	54	28.3
(V-) MP	5	41	55	37.4	8	35	58	37.7	5	34	61	34.9

a. Low = compulsory primary and lower secondary school, med. = medium, upper secondary school; high = university college or university (started or completed degree).
b. Member survey is from 1991.
c. There was no delegate survey in 1989.
d. The Liberal Party was not represented in Parliament from 1989–1993, and only had two MPs in the periods 2001–2005 and 2009–2013.

Table 6A.3. Occupation congruence in 1989–2009 by party: percentage shares of different occupation categories.[a] Party voters (V) compared to party members (M), delegates (D), and MPs[bcde]

	W	WCL	WCM	WCH	PI	SE	S	P	H
					1990				
Voters									
SV	14.8	19.5	25.7	11.4	1.4	4.3	7.6	11	4.3
Ap	22.2	16.2	10.7	5.4	2.2	5.4	3.8	26.1	8
Sp	12.5	15.4	8.7	7.7	29.8	4.8	2.9	12.5	5.8
KrF	6.4	10.8	16.6	10.8	5.7	5.7	2.5	31.2	10.2
V	10.7	13.3	21.3	16	2.7	6.7	10.7	16	2.7
H	11.4	12.7	19.4	15.5	1.3	9.8	7.8	14.8	7.3
FrP	26.6	13.8	7.4	10.8	3	6.4	8.4	17.2	6.4
Members									
SV	6.5	8.6	29.2	11.2	2.9	4.4	26	10.6	0.6
Ap	20.2	13.9	7.5	8.6	4.5	3.7	8.6	31.1	1.9
Sp	6.2	6.2	6.2	6.2	37.4	2.6	4.4	24.9	5.9
KrF	7.9	7.9	19.1	6.5	8.3	4.3	2.5	37.9	5.4
V	5.9	9.4	28.3	14.2	3.9	8.3	11.4	16.1	2.4
H	6.6	8.1	12.8	22.3	1.9	19.4	2.8	22.7	3.3
FrP	16.2	12.9	6.7	9	3.8	11.4	23.3	13.8	2.9
MPs									
SV	5.9	0	35.3	41.2	0	5.9	5.9	0	5.9
Ap	4.8	12.7	31.7	39.7	6.3	1.6	3.2	0	0
Sp	0	0	9.1	45.5	36.4	0	0	0	9.1
KrF	0	0	35.7	35.7	7.1	7.1	0	0	14.3
V	n.a.	n.a.	n.a.	n.a.	n.a.	n.a.	n.a.	n.a.	n.a.
H	0	2.7	18.9	51.4	13.5	8.1	2.7	0	2.7
FrP	0	0	13.6	50	0	31.8	0	4.5	0
					2000				
Voters									
SV	8.7	14.3	37.7	5.2	0.9	1.3	16	13.9	2.2
Ap	14.2	15	27.8	6.2	0.8	3.4	4.2	26.9	1.4
Sp	12.9	11.8	17.2	3.2	19.4	4.3	4.3	20.4	6.5
KrF	12.7	14.1	21.6	7	1.9	3.8	5.2	28.6	5.2
V	5.7	5.7	47.1	11.4	2.9	4.3	7.1	12.9	2.9
H	6.8	13.6	27.5	16	0.9	8.2	7	16.9	3.1
FrP	15	14.4	14.4	4.2	0.6	4.8	5.4	39.5	1.8

(*continued*)

Table 6A.3.   *Continued*

	W	WCL	WCM	WCH	PI	SE	S	P	H
Members									
SV	9.3	5.6	42.6	14.8	1.9	5.6	13	7.4	
Ap	19.6	5	13.7	8.3	2	2	8.7	37.4	3.4
Sp	11.5	4.8	12.9	7.7	31.1	6.2	0.5	23.4	1.9
KrF	7.3	3.5	20.1	9.7	4.9	3.5	7.3	37.8	5.9
V	6.7	4.4	26.7	15.6	2.2	11.1	6.7	24.4	2.2
H	6	2.2	16.1	15.6	3.8	18.3	7.4	29	1.6
FrP	25.6	4.4	10	7.8	1.1	16.7	5.6	27.8	1.1
Delegates									
SV	10.7	7.1	35.7	21.4	0		17.9	7.1	0
Ap	16.5	7.8	22.2	25.1	3	4.3	11.6	9.5	0
Sp	6.2	3.8	17.5	23.8	13.8	16.2	15	3.8	0
KrF	5.9	4	27.7	30.7	1	6.9	12.9	9.9	1
V	3.6	0	32.1	28.6	3.6	10.7	17.9	3.6	0
H	4.9	1.6	27	22.1	1.6	14.8	13.9	12.3	1.6
FrP	15.9	6.1	20.7	23.2	0	18.3	3.7	11	1.2
MPs									
SV	4.3	8.7	26.1	43.5	0	4.3	13	0	0
Ap	9.5	9.5	26.2	35.7	2.4	4.8	11.9	0	0
Sp	0	0	40	40	20	0	0	0	0
KrF	0	0	45.5	45.5	0	4.5	0	0	4.5
V	n.a.	n.a.	n.a.	n.a.	n.a.	n.a.	n.a.	n.a.	n.a.
H	0	0	31.6	52.6	2.6	5.3	7.9	0	0
FrP	11.5	15.4	19.2	34.6	3.8	15.4	0	0	0
					2010				
Voters									
SV	5.9	16.1	44.9	5.1	0	0.8	14.4	12.7	0
Ap	9	15.1	31.7	8	0.6	2.9	8.4	23.7	0.6
Sp	13.5	4.2	27.1	4.2	16.7	7.3	9.4	17.7	0
KrF	3	12.1	30.3	12.1	0	6.1	9.1	25.8	1.5
V	1.6	6.2	32.8	14.1	0	7.8	15.6	21.9	0
H	5.6	9.4	36.2	16	1	5.6	4.9	19.5	1.7
FrP	17.6	8.1	17.6	7.7	0.7	8.1	4	33.3	2.9

	W	WCL	WCM	WCH	PI	SE	S	P	H
Members									
SV	7.6	4.7	38.6	12.9	1.8	6.4	5.8	21.6	0.6
Ap	14.6	4.9	15.9	11.7	0.8	4.6	5.1	41.6	0.8
Sp	8.7	3.3	15.7	8.4	20.6	6.8	1.1	35.5	
KrF	6.9	3.1	20.6	6.6	1.7	7.1	1.7	49.8	2.6
V	8.3	3	28.8	12.9	3	12.1	4.5	27.3	
H	5.3	2.2	15.2	16.3	2.6	19.6	1.1	35.5	2
FrP	18.5	2.2	9.1	5.3	1.9	15.8	3.1	42.4	1.7
Delegates									
SV	10.7	7.1	35.7	21.4	0	0	17.9	7.1	0
Ap	16.5	7.8	22.2	25.1	3	4.3	11.6	9.5	0
Sp	6.2	3.8	17.5	23.8	13.8	16.2	15	3.8	0
KrF	5.9	4	27.7	30.7	1	6.9	12.9	9.9	1
V	3.6	0	32.1	28.6	3.6	10.7	17.9	3.6	0
H	4.9	1.6	27	22.1	1.6	14.8	13.9	12.3	1.6
FrP	15.9	6.1	20.7	23.2	0	18.3	3.7	11	1.2
MPs									
SV	0	20	20	60	0	0	0	0	0
Ap	8.1	1.6	19.4	58.1	1.6	3.2	8.1	0	0
Sp	0	9.1	9.1	27.3	27.3	18.2	0	0	9.1
KrF	0	0	0	80	0	10	10	0	0
V	n.a.	n.a.	n.a.	n.a.	n.a.	n.a.	n.a.	n.a.	n.a.
H	0	3.3	26.7	43.3	3.3	6.7	16.7	0	0
FrP	7.3	9.8	26.8	39	2.4	7.3	4.9	0	2.4

a. Occupation (or source of subsistence): Worker (W) = ordinary and trained worker, craftsman etc.; White-collar low (WCL) = subordinated level (shop assistants, clerk etc.); White-collar medium (WCM) = mid-level (teacher, nurse, engineer etc.); White-collar high (WCH) = superior/chief position at mid- or top-level in public or private unit; Primary industry (PI) (farmers, fishermen etc.); Self-employed (SE) (company owners, independent professionals like dentists, lawyers etc.); Pensioners (P); Students (S); Homemakers (H).

b. Member survey is from 1991.

c. There was no delegate survey in 1989.

d. The Liberal Party was not represented in Parliament from 1989–1993, and only had two MPs in the periods 2001–2005 and 2009–2013.

Table 6A.4. Sector congruence in 1989–2009 by party: percentage shares of different sector affiliations[a] and Gallagher's disproportionality index (GDI): party voters (V) compared to party members (M), delegates (D), and MPs[b]

	1990				2000				2010			
SV	Priv.	Pub.	Org.	GDI	Priv.	Pub.	Org.	GDI	Priv.	Pub.	Org.	GDI
Voters	36	63	1		36	59	5		25	71	5	
(V-) M	24	72	4	10.8	18	75	7	17.1	23	71	6	1.6
(V-) D[c]	n.a.	n.a.	n.a.	n.a.	15	71	14	18.3	21	63	16	10
(V-) MP	27	53	20	16.5	30	50	20	13.1	20	50	30	23.4

	1990				2000				2010			
Ap	Priv.	Pub.	Org.	GDI	Priv.	Pub.	Org.	GDI	Priv.	Pub.	Org.	GDI
Voters	50	46	4		50	46	5		44	54	2	
(V-) M	48	45	7	2.7	42	50	9	6.9	42	49	9	6.2
(V-) D[c]	n.a.	n.a.	n.a.	n.a.	25	56	20	21.8	32	51	17	13.8
(V-) MP	25	54	21	22.1	30	51	19	17.6	19	49	32	27.8

	1990				2000				2010			
Sp	Priv.	Pub.	Org.	GDI	Priv.	Pub.	Org.	GDI	Priv.	Pub.	Org.	GDI
Voters	55	34	11		55	39	7		36	60	4	
(V-) M	76	19	5	18.7	58	36	7	3	65	29	6	30.1
(V-) D[c]	n.a.	n.a.	n.a.	n.a.	32	43	26	21.3	39	43	18	15.7
(V-) MP	50	40	10	5.6	40	40	20	14.1	60	30	10	27.5

	1990				2000				2010			
KrF	Priv.	Pub.	Org.	GDI	Priv.	Pub.	Org.	GDI	Priv.	Pub.	Org.	GDI
Voters	39	57	4		58	38	4		39	46	15	
(V-) M	40	52	7	4.2	37	56	7	19.7	45	46	10	5.5
(V-) D[c]	n.a.	n.a.	n.a.	n.a.	27	60	13	27.6	28	57	15	11
(V-) MP	17	75	8	20.3	5	60	35	46.1	22	33	44	25.5

	1990				2000				2010			
V	Priv.	Pub.	Org.	GDI	Priv.	Pub.	Org.	GDI	Priv.	Pub.	Org.	GDI
Voters	44	52	4		35	59	6		34	60	6	
(V-) M	33	65	2	12.1	38	61	2	3.8	46	50	4	11.1
(V-) D[c]	n.a.	n.a.	n.a.	n.a.	34	53	14	7.1	39	48	13	10.4
(V-) MP[d]	n.a.	n.a.	n.a.	n.a.	0	100	0	38.4	0	100	0	37.4

H	1990				2000				2010			
	Priv.	Pub.	Org.	GDI	Priv.	Pub.	Org.	GDI	Priv.	Pub.	Org.	GDI
Voters	55	41	4		70	28	2		65	31	5	
(V-) M	70	27	3	14.5	66	33	2	4.5	66	31	3	1.6
(V-) Dᶜ	n.a.	n.a.	n.a.	n.a.	48	39	13	19.1	54	39	7	9.7
(V-) MP	63	23	14	15.6	23	57	20	41.1	36	40	24	25.3

FrP	1990				2000				2010			
	Priv.	Pub.	Org.	GDI	Priv.	Pub.	Org.	GDI	Priv.	Pub.	Org.	GDI
Voters	74	25	2		72	26	3		76	24	1	
(V-) M	77	21	2	3.5	74	23	3	2.6	76	20	3	3.2
(V-) Dᶜ	n.a.	n.a.	n.a.	n.a.	64	28	9	7.2	60	30	10	13.7
(V-) MP	43	43	14	26.7	52	28	20	18.6	42	26	32	32.6

[a] Employees in the private sector, public sector, and in various organizations; pensioners, students, and housewives are excluded.
[b] Member survey is from 1991.
[c] There was no delegate survey in 1989.
[d] The Liberal Party was not represented in Parliament from 1989–1993, and only had two MPs in the periods 2001–2005 and 2009–2013.

NOTES

1. See, e.g., classics like Milbrath (1965) and Putnam (1976).

2. For a similar discussion on measuring issue congruence along different scales (the problem that the same mean in two different groups can be the result of quite different distributions), see chapter 7.

3. It should be noted that we have not excluded the MP from Aune-Lista/FFF in 1989, and the MP from Kystpartiet in 1989 in the description of party MPs in general.

4. The exception is left and new left parties in the 1970s and early 1980s.

5. Member and delegate figures have been weighted by the number of party members in each party to take into account variation in party size (see the discussion in chapter 4). For the N's, see table 4.5. There was no delegate survey in 1989.

6. See http://www.ssb.no/en/statistikkbanken.

7. If we change the share of highly educated voters to 30 percent, the GDI scores become 14.6 (V-M), 32.4 (V-D), and 37.7 (V-MP), respectively.

8. It should be noted that the category "white-collar high" includes only top-level chief positions (like senior government officials and general managers) in the voter surveys, while mid-level senior positions are most likely included in others.

7

Policy Representation

If democracy is perceived as the implementation of people's will, issue agreement between the electorate and representatives is crucial. In chapter 2, we argued that policy congruence between voters and members and voters and delegates would testify to the parties' ability to channel preferences through the party organization. On the basis of the literature arguing that weakened mass parties mean weakened representative capacity of parties, we hypothesized that the preferences of both party members and delegates have become less congruent with the policy views of voters over the last decades, and that the issue congruence between party voters and party MPs has also declined. In this chapter, we explore these claims empirically. Following the expectation that membership decline is an essential factor for this development, one would also expect that the parties that have experienced the steepest decrease in membership figures have become most detached from the voters. As discussed in chapter 4, these are the Labour Party, Centre Party, Christian People's Party, and the Conservative Party in Norway.

We first offer a short review of earlier research on policy congruence in Norway. Then, we describe different methodological approaches to the study of issue congruence. We discuss strengths and weaknesses of the different measures and end up with three measures to use in the analysis, which we believe complement each other. The main part of the chapter is a longitudinal empirical study on issue congruence between voters and members, voters and delegates, and voters and MPs along several ideological dimensions—issues based on cleavages that have been constitutional for parties and still important for people's vote choice (e.g., Valen and Rokkan 1974; Karlsen and Aardal 2011). In representational terms, it is on these issues that congruence should be particularly high.

PREVIOUS RESEARCH ON ISSUE CONGRUENCE IN NORWAY

Studies of issue congruence has typically and naturally centered on the relationship between voters and MPs. There are no previous studies of issue congruence between voters and party members in Norway. Although several studies have focused on issue congruence between voters and MPs in the context of Norwegian politics, few have assessed the level of congruence per se. One exception is a comparative study of the Nordic countries from the mid-1990s by Holmberg (2000). He found that issue congruence between voters and MPs in Norway is on level with the other Nordic countries, and concluded that the representative process works as it creates issue agreement, at least to some degree (ibid., 170). Moreover, the parties on the right tended to fare worse than the other parties (ibid., 159). Members of parliament in the conservative and progress parties were positioned clearly to the right of their voters on economic issues. However, the immigration issue showed a more improved congruence for these parties.

Three other studies based on Norwegian data focus on the relationship between voters and MPs, but do not assess the level of congruence per se. Narud and Skare (1999) reexamine May's law using data from the early 1990s. They find that the curvilinear patterns predicted by May exist, but only in about one third of the cases they examine. They are not able, however, to see any meaningful patterns in the cases where the party activists are more extreme than voters and MPs. In an article from 2007, Narud and Valen find that representatives are more extreme than voters (Narud and Valen 2007a). In their book on the representativeness of the Norwegian Storting, Matthews and Valen (1999, 128) conclude that although parties provide linkages between voters and governments, the congruence is not always strong. Overall, we would still characterize the congruence they found as relatively good. Congruence between MPs and voters is relatively good, and the total distributions reveal similar patterns for voters and MPs when they are reported (e.g., Narud and Valen 2007a, 310).

In sum, the studies in the context of Norwegian politics mirror the tendencies in the wider literature. There is agreement between MPs and voters on important policy issues at least to some degree, and individuals at higher levels in the party hierarchy tend to agree with each other to a greater extent than individuals at lower levels (Narud and Skare 1999; Narud and Valen 2007a).[1] Nobody has so far studied the development of issue congruence in Norway over time, be it between voters and members, voters and delegates, or voters and MPs.

MEASURING ISSUE CONGRUENCE

Measuring issue congruence involves the comparison of the preferences of voters to the preferences of members, delegates, and MPs. This type of issue congruence is often studied by comparing measures of central tendencies, the mean or the median.

These are intuitive measures that mostly offer a nice description of the main tendencies in the distribution. However, for less unified groups, these measures may result in considerable loss of information (Pierce 1999, 14; Andeweg 2011, 41): The same mean in two different groups can be the result of quite different distributions. For example, extreme polarization can produce the same mean as a normal distribution. Hence, although the mean is a good point of departure, it is necessary to apply other measures that address the problem of distribution.

In a recent influential article, Golder and Stramski (2010) suggest to compare the total distribution to measure many-to-many relationships:

$$\text{CONGRUENCE (MANY-TO-MANY)} = XF_1\ (x) - F_2\ (x)$$

$F_1(x)$ and $F_2(x)$ are the cumulative distribution of functions for the two groups compared. Essentially, this measure captures the area between the two groups' (cumulative) graphs. If the preferences of the two groups are identically distributed the area between the graphs will be zero, and congruence will be perfect (Golder and Stramski 2010, 96). According to Andeweg (2011, 43), Golder and Stramski (2010) offer no compelling reason for using the *cumulative* distribution function. He suggests that we should rather, at each point on the scale used, compare the percentage of the two groups who position themselves on that point. For each point, the lowest number should be picked and summarized. The sum will be the "common area under the graphs" (CoAr) for the two groups compared (see figure 7.1 for an example).

Measures that take the total distribution of preferences into account also have problems. High scores rely on the two groups compared, placing themselves on the exact same point on the scale. Hence, it is likely that the more points there are on a

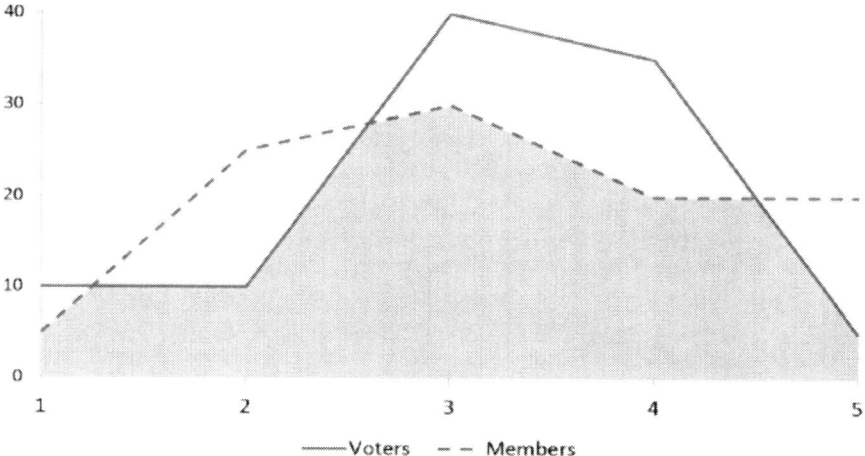

Figure 7.1. The common area under the graph (CoAr) (Adapted from Andeweg 2011, 44).

scale, the less likely it is that congruence score will be high. For example, the commonly used 11-point left-right scale may result in less congruence than five-point Likert scales. Moreover, if all the MPs/delegates/members totally agree (1), and all the voters somewhat agree (2) on a five-point Likert scale, the common area under the graph will be zero, implying shockingly bad representation. Although this might be a somewhat unlikely scenario, the point is that representation is not (just) about similar distributions. One could argue that it is enough that two groups agree (or disagree) with a statement for their preference to be congruent, that the extent they disagree or agree is of less importance as the difference between agreeing and disagreeing is more fundamental than the difference between totally agreeing and somewhat agreeing, or totally disagreeing and somewhat disagreeing. Holmberg (e.g., 2011) uses what he calls a measure of policy agreement in much of his work on political representation. This is the absolute difference between the proportion of MPs that agrees with the statement and the proportion of voters that agrees with the statement.

We suggest a similar measure to Holmberg's: the Agree index (AI). First, we calculate the absolute difference between the share of voters that agree with an issue and the proportion of members/delegates/MPs that agree. Then, we add the absolute difference between the proportion of the voters that disagree and the proportion of the members/delegates/MPs that disagree, and subtract this sum from 100.[2] This means that a score of 100 indicates complete agreement, and a score of −100 indicates complete disagreement between the two groups compared. The advantage of this measure is that it complements the mean and the CoAr by emphasizing the fundamental difference between agreeing and disagreeing with a policy proposal.

To sum up, in this chapter, we rely on three different measures of issue congruence that we believe will offer a reliable expression of congruence. First, we use the difference in mean. This measure shows the central tendency in the material, and is a very intuitive measure. Our main measure is the common area under the graph (CoAr). The advantage of this measure is that it takes the total distribution into account. If the CoAr score is high, then issue congruence is good without a doubt. However, if the CoAr index is low, we know that the total distribution between the two groups varies, but as discussed, congruence may be good. To control for this, we also utilize the Agree index accounted for above. The advantage of this measure (AI) is that it emphasizes the fundamental difference between two groups when it comes to agreeing and disagreeing with a statement.

What is high and what is low congruence? Everything close to perfect congruence should be considered high congruence. For example, Andeweg (2011) calls a CoAr score of 89 on the left-right scale between Dutch parliamentarians and voters almost perfect. In Andeweg's study, the CoAr index varies between 55 and 89 for the whole of parliament, but was considerably lower in the analysis of individual parties (Andeweg 2011, 48).

The Agree index is not utilized in earlier studies, so in order to "test" the reliability of the Agree index and the CoAr index we have compared the scores of voters and members and voters and MPs belonging to different parties, e.g., voters from the

Socialist Left and members from Progress. The scores are considerably lower when we mix party affiliation. For the immigration issue in 2010, the CoAr index is 28 and the Agree index is –32 for SV (voters) and FrP (members), while it is 29 (CoAr) and –25 (AI) for SV (voters) and FrP (MPs).[3] This is expected as the Socialist Left Party and the Progress Party are the main opponents on this issue. Ap and the Conservatives do not differ that much on this issue, and both the CoAr and Agree index is 75 for voters (Ap) and members (H). However, the scores for the AP-H relationship are much lower when it comes to reducing taxes on high incomes, an issue where the two parties are the traditional main opponents. The CoAr index is 54 and the Agree index only 24 for Ap-voters and H-members, and for the relationship between A-voters and H-MPs the CoAr index is 37 and the Agree index is –21. These low numbers can be compared to the relatively high scores presented in the analysis below, and imply that the measures indeed give a reliable indication of the congruence between two groups. As a general rule, a score of more than 70 should be considered relatively high.

We will, as a rule, report all three measures for the analysis where we study congruence for the sum of parties. In the analysis by party, we mostly report the CoAr index, but we will report in the text if any of the other two measures show different results.

DATA MATERIAL

Our data consist of surveys on voters, members, delegates, and MPs for three different points in time around 1990 (1988–1993), around 2000 (2000–2001), and around 2010 (2009 and 2012). The surveys were not undertaken as a joint research project, so the number of comparable questions differs somehow. We have the best data for 2009, with seven identical questions asked to voters, members, delegates, and MPs.

Table 7.1. Data used to study political congruence between voters and members, delegates, and MPs[a]

	Voters	*Members*	*Delegates*	*MPs*
1990	NES 1989 and NES 1993	Member survey 1991	No data	MP Survey 1988 MP Survey 1993
2000	NES 2001	Member survey 2000	Delegate survey 2000	MP Survey 2000 and MP Survey 2005
2010	NES 2009 and citizen survey 2009	Member survey 2009	Delegate survey 2009	MP Survey 2012

a. See chapter 4 for details.

In 2000, only three questions are similar at all levels, and in 1990, we do not have any identical questions for voters, members, and MPs. In this case, the strategy is to use some questions to measure the issue congruence between voters and members, and other questions to study congruence between voters and MPs. In addition, in 1990, to get identical questions, we must compare the NES 1989 data to the member survey 1991 and the NES 1993 to the MP survey in 1993. This is not ideal, but it nevertheless offers an account of the level of issue congruence, although the results will not be totally comparable.

We mostly use different questions (wordings) for each point in time, but items tapping the same underlying issue dimensions. This is partly necessary due to variations in the formulations used in the surveys we compare. Relevant policy questions differ within fields from one year to the next so it has been necessary for the investigators to develop new formulations over a period of twenty years within the same time series. Because of this, we must be careful with the interpretations. Differences over time may be down to the different wordings of questions, resulting in different congruence patterns. However, two questions have been asked in exactly the same way to voters and to party members at all three points in time. In the analysis, we use these two questions to study the congruence between voters and members longitudinally.

Some minor problems should be kept in mind when surveys based on different types of groups are compared. First, different types of data collection are used. The national election surveys are based on face to face or telephone interviews, while the data for members, delegates, and members of parliament are based on postal surveys. Hence, in the voter surveys, the middle category (neither nor) is not presented to the respondents. However, in a postal survey, the middle category is necessarily presented, and we should expect a greater proportion of members, delegates, and MPs in this category. In 2009, to maximize the numbers of comparable questions, we conducted a national representative voter survey in addition to the national election surveys. TNS Gallup, who conducted the 2009 citizen survey on behalf of the research group, as a rule also presents the middle category to the respondents. As expected, a larger proportion of respondents placed themselves on the middle category in this data file as compared to that in the 2009 national election survey. We use the national election surveys when we study congruence over time to make the analysis comparable. However, in the last empirical analysis, when we focus on the representational capacity of the parties today, we use the Gallup data for all questions to compare all seven issue dimensions on equal terms.[4]

EMPIRICAL ANALYSIS

In this section, we study political congruence between voters and three other levels in the political parties—members, delegates, and MPs—for the period 1990–2010. We begin by investigating the three issue dimensions over time. However, as accounted for above, we do not have identical questions for all levels for all three points in time. Therefore, in this first analysis, the emphasis will be on overall congruence and representation, and we will disregard smaller differences. In the second part, we focus on the relationship between voters and members. Two identical questions have been asked to voters and members in 1990, 2000, and in 2010. This makes it possible to study changes in congruence more accurately. This analysis will offer a more precise account of whether or not the congruence between voters and members has decreased over time. In the third part, we study representation today by examining issue congruence between voters and members, voters and delegates, and voters and MPs on a total of seven issue dimensions.

In chapter 2, we accounted for the distinction between studying representation by individual parties and the parties in sum. We do not believe there is a right way or a wrong way in normative terms. However, the increasing volatility at the voter level has perhaps increased the need to study representation as the sum of parties (cf. Andeweg 2011). Hence, in the empirical analysis, we first study the entire party sphere—how well all members, delegates, and MPs represent voters. In these analyses, we will weigh the member and delegate data based on the parties' proportion of total members.[5] Second, we study congruence and representation by party—how well party members, delegates, and MPs of a specific party represent their voters.

Voters, Members, Delegates, and MPs

Do party members, delegates, and members of parliament represent the voters as a whole? Has this representation declined during the past two decades? Table 7.2 presents the results of the congruence analyses between voters and members, voters and delegates, and voters and MPs in 1990, 2000, and 2010 on three essential policy dimensions in Norwegian electoral politics: economy, environmental, and immigration/morality issues. The first issue represents an old traditional political cleavage, while the latter two are more recent conflicts and are often referred to as new politics. In this table, we include all the three measures accounted for above. As noted above, small differences in congruence should not be emphasized.

The analysis reveals relatively high congruence between voters and members, voters and delegates, and voters and MPs for all the three points in time. For voters and members, the CoAr index and the AI mostly score around 80–90, and this must be considered high, as a score of 100 indicates perfect congruence or perfect agreement. All three measures also show the same main pattern. There is no clear trend toward less congruence over time, although on all three issues, it appears that congruence between members and voters have decreased somehow. However, the differences are small; the different wording of the questions can account for these small differences.

It is somewhat less problematic to compare between levels in the party. In most of cases, we use identical questions. Congruence between voters and members tend to be better than congruence between voters and MPs. This pattern fits well with the finding in the congruence literature that polarization seems to be increasing at higher levels in the party hierarchy (e.g., Widfeldt 1999a). The exception is the morality dimension in 2000. Conversely, in this case, we use a somewhat different question for members than for voters and MPs (see the notes under the table). As voters and MPs were asked identical questions, it is expected that congruence should be higher in this case.

Table 7.2. Issue congruence between voters and party members, delegates, and MPs 1990, 2000, and 2010. The difference in mean (DM), the common area under the graph (CoAr), and the Agree index (AI)

	1990			2000			2010		
	DM	CoAr	AI	DM	CoAr	AI	DM	CoAr	AI
Economy[a]									
Voters-Members	0.1	90	85	0.1	84	87	0.3	80	79
Voters-Delegates	n.a.	n.a.	n.a.	0.1	79	93	0.1	78	61
Voters-MPs	0.5	79	70	0.8	70	78	0.3	75	82
Environment[b]									
Voters-Members	0.2	87	89	0.5	85	83	0.5	83	77
Voters-Delegates	n.a.	n.a.	n.a.	0.3	78	83	0.1	85	84
Voters-MPs	0.4	88	89	0.9	63	66	0.7	69	54
Morality/immigration[c]									
Voters-Members	0.1	84	87	0.7	69	55	0.1	80	83
Voters-Delegates	n.a.	n.a.	n.a.	0.4	79	74	1.1	59	42
Voters-MPs	n.a	n.a	n.a.	0.1	77	66	0.7	75	66

a. Q2010: High incomes should be taxed harder. Q2000: It is more important to develop public services than to reduce taxation. Q1990: V-M, V-D: To exhort people to greater effort, we should be willing to accept bigger differences in wage levels. V-MPs: Reduce taxes on high incomes (Voters) (Very good, and so forth) reduce taxes (MPs) (totally agree, and so forth).

b. Q2010: We should develop gas-power plants in Norway even though CO_2 cleaning is not possible with today's technology. Q2000: We should develop gas-power plants in Norway. Q1990: V-M: We should develop cleaning plants for discharge/waste from private households, industry, and agriculture even if this means higher taxes.

c. Q2010: Immigration is a serious threat to our national character. Q2000: Aim for a society where Christian values play a bigger role than today (voters and MPs); We should work to strengthen the role Christian morality plays in society (members and delegates). Q1990: V-M: We should increase the economic support to immigrants so that they can preserve their own culture.

The analyses so far show that members, delegates, and representatives represent voters fairly well, and that there is no clear tendency toward decreasing congruence. Is this also true for the individual parties? In what follows, we study issue congruence on the three issue dimensions presented above by party. Table 7.3 presents the CoAr index related to tax-issues between voters and members, voters and delegates, and voters and MPs by party. We will report in the text if any of the other measures report different results than the CoAr index.

On the whole, table 7.3 reports good congruence between the parties' voters and members, voters and delegates, and voters and MPs.[6] On average, there is no general trend toward decreasing congruence at any level. There are clear differences between the parties, but the differences vary over time. For example, in 1990, voter-member congruence was best for the Conservative and the Progress parties. In 2000, the parties on the left—Ap, SV, and Sp—had the strongest degree of congruence. Consequently, we find little support for the hypothesis that the parties that have lost most members have experienced a steep decrease in congruence. The differences between parties are most likely due to the different questions (i.e. formulations) used than on any tendencies toward better or worse representation for the parties involved.

Table 7.3. Issue congruence between voters and members, delegates, and MPs: Economy 1990–2010. CoAr index[a]

	1990s			2000s			2010s		
	V-M	V-D	V-MP	V-M	V-D	V-MP	V-M	V-D	V-MP
SV	67	n.a.	53	86	67	53	75	63	35
Ap	75	n.a.	69	83	78	60	75	72	76
Sp	79	n.a.	75	83	78	38	80	84	64
KrF	78	n.a.	52	81	82	28	69	78	48
V	59	n.a.	n.a.	81	71	n.a.	80	68	n.a.
H	85	n.a.	43	72	58	56	77	57	72
FrP	85	n.a.	13	69	47	71	81	54	65
Average	75	n.a.	44	79	69	51	77	68	60

a. Q2010: Higher incomes should be taxed harder.
Q2000: It is more important to develop public services than to reduce taxation.
Q1990: V-M: To exhort people to greater effort, we should be willing to accept bigger differences in wage levels. V-MPs: Voters: Reduce taxes on high incomes (a very good idea, and so forth). MPs: Reduce taxes (totally agree, and so forth).

The results also confirm the impression from the first analysis that congruence between voters and members is better than congruence between voters and representatives. Mostly, delegates fall somewhere in between.

Table 7.4. Congruence between voters and members, delegates, MPs: Environmental issues 1990–2010. CoAr index[a]

	1990s			2000s			2010s		
	V-M	V-D	V-MP	V-M	V-D	V-MP	V-M	V-D	V-MP
SV	93	n.a.	55	57	51	66	93	74	70
Ap	91	n.a.	67	81	49	49	79	79	82
Sp	82	n.a.	49	81	77	71	88	86	63
KrF	87	n.a.	74	76	34	74	86	75	44
V	97	n.a.	n.a.	67	72	0	83	62	n.a
H	83	n.a.	68	88	74	56	69	75	57
FrP	68	n.a.	69	92	71	46	71	55	41
Average	86	n.a.	64	77	61	52	81	72	60

a. Q2010: We should develop gas-power plants in Norway even though CO_2 cleaning is not possible with today's technology.
Q2000: We should develop gas-power plants in Norway.
Q1990: V-M: We should develop cleaning plants for discharge/waste from private households, industry, and agriculture even if this means higher taxes. V-MP: Environmental issue dimension 10-point scale.

Much of the same pattern found in table 7.2 is found in table 7.3 and table 7.4, which reports congruence by party for environmental issues and immigration/morality issues. Overall, it is good congruence, but it differs somewhat between parties. There is no clear pattern with regard to the differences. For example, SV's level of congruence is high in 1990, then low in 2000, and high again in 2010. The AI is also low in 2000 (38). One explanation could be that the party did positively during the 2001 election, and a number of former Labour voters opted for the party. These voters shared the parties' views on environmental issues to a lesser extent than voters who voted for the party in 1989 and 2009 (Aardal 2003).

Again, congruence is best between voters and members and lowest for voters and MPs. Above, we saw that for the morality issue in 2000, congruence was better between voters and MPs than between voters and members. We do not find the same result in this analysis, and this is mostly due to the extremely low congruence between the voters and MPs of the Centre Party.[7]

Table 7.5. **Issue congruence by party 1990–2010. Immigration (1990, 2010) and morality (2000). CoAr index[a]**

	1990s			2000s			2010s		
	V-M	V-D	V-MP	V-M	V-D	V-MP	V-M	V-D	V-MP
SV	69	n.a.	n.a.	65	54	67	85	75	75
Ap	81	n.a.	n.a.	75	72	59	76	50	44
Sp	80	n.a.	n.a.	72	76	9	77	65	60
KrF	80	n.a.	n.a.	67	82	73	80	64	61
V	77	n.a.	n.a.	83	74	n.a.	74	49	n.a.
H	82	n.a.	n.a.	58	68	81	79	61	63
FrP	83	n.a.	n.a.	78	76	90	83	76	72
Average	79	n.a.	n.a.	71	72	63	79	63	63

a. Q 2010: Immigration is a serious threat to our national identity.
Q 2000: V-M, V-D: We should work to strengthen the role Christian morality plays in society. V-MP: Aim for a society where Christian values play a bigger role than today.
Q 1990: V-M: We should increase the economic support to immigrants so that they can preserve their own culture.

So far, the results indicate that parties still represent voters on important issues, and there is no indication that members have removed themselves from voters. Congruence between voters and members is better than congruence between voters and MPs.

Congruence between Voters and Members over Time

Two questions have been asked to both voters and party members in the three points in time we study. These questions allow us to study the relationship between voters and members over time in more detail. Both questions deal with economic issues related to taxes and the difference in wage levels. These issues are just as relevant today as they were 20–30 years ago. In what follows, we first report the total congruence for both items, and then study congruence by party. Figures 7.2 and 7.3 show the differences in mean, the common area under the graph, and the Agree index for all voters and members.

Figure 7.2 indicates good congruence between voters and members for all the three points in time. There is a slight tendency toward increasing congruence. All

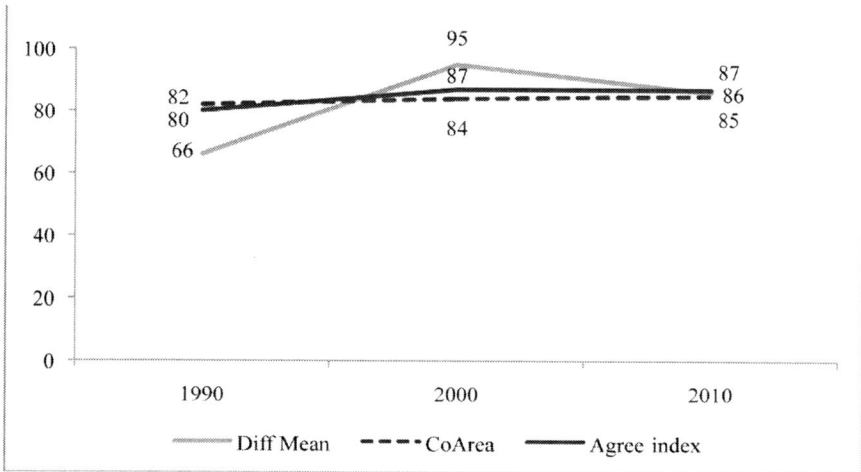

Figure 7.2.   Congruence between voters and members in 1990–2010. Better to develop the public sector than reduce taxation.[8]

three measures indicate slightly better congruence in 2000 and 2010 than in 1990. The same main pattern is found in figure 7.3, which reports congruence based on the statement, "We should accept greater income differences."

Overall, all the three measures indicate good congruence between voters and members. However, the CoAr index indicates somewhat decreasing congruence from 1990 to 2010, as it decreases from 87 in 1990 to 78 in 2010. On the other hand, the

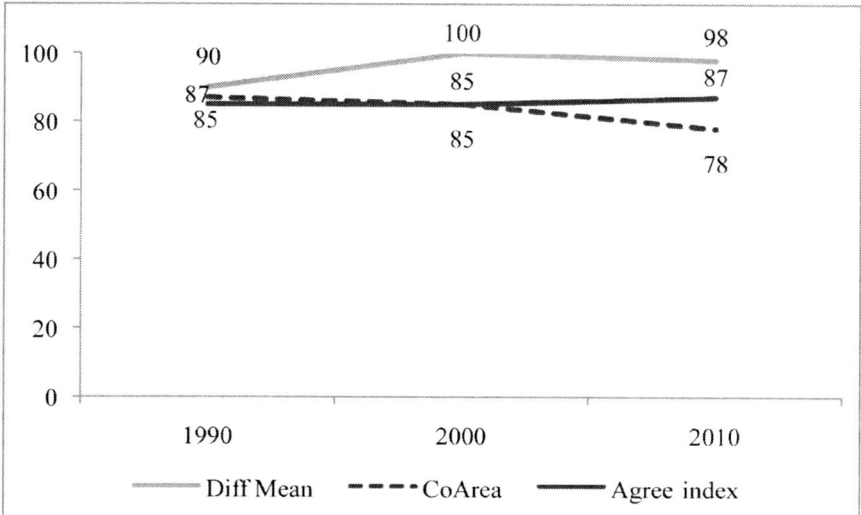

Figure 7.3.   Congruence between voters and members 1990–2010. Accept greater income differences.[9]

AI increases from 85 in 1990 to 87 in 2010. The differences in mean also indicate better congruence in 2000 and 2010 than in 1990. In fact, the DM indicates perfect congruence in 2000, and nearly perfect congruence in 2010. The main reason why the measurements differ somewhat is that in 2010, although 55 percent of both voters and members disagree with the proposition, members totally disagree to a greater extent. This results in a lower CoAr index than Agree index. Nevertheless, in sum they show that on the whole, party members represent the policy views of the electorate to a great extent for the whole period covered.

Now, we turn to congruence by party. Table 7.6 shows congruence between voters and members by party for the question, "It is better to develop public services than to reduce taxation." On average, the results resemble the analysis of the party sphere as a whole: congruence between voters and party members is good, and has increased somewhat since the 1990s. For the whole period, there is a difference between four of the parties that have extremely good congruence—SV, Ap, Sp, and KrF. On the one hand, the two parties on the right, the Conservatives and the Progress Party, have less congruence. The reason for the relatively low level of congruence for the Progress Party is that the voters are more inclined than the members to say that it is better to develop the public sector than to reduce taxes.[10] To a lesser extent, this is also the case for the Conservative Party. This means that the parties that have lost most members do not stand out among parties with (most) decreasing or particularly low levels of congruence. This pattern does not fit the expected party differences based on the party decline literature.

Table 7.6. Congruence between voters and members after party affiliation/choice. Better to develop the public sector than to reduce taxation[a]

	1990s			2000s			2010s		
	DM	*CoA*	*AI*	*DM*	*CoA*	*AI*	*DM*	*CoA*	*AI*
SV	0.4	77	88	0.3	86	86	0.2	87	93
Ap	0.2	83	87	0.2	83	89	0.1	82	93
Sp	0.2	80	82	0.2	83	82	0.1	90	93
KrF	0.2	82	82	0.0	81	81	0.4	76	84
V	0.6	70	67	0.2	81	83	0.1	88	88
H	0.6	76	62	0.4	72	74	0.6	64	61
FrP	1.3	63	31	0.6	69	64	0.8	64	47
Average	0.5	76	71	0.3	79	80	0.3	79	80

a. Q: It is better to develop public services than to reduce taxation.

The main tendency in table 7.6 is that good and slightly increasing congruence is also found related to the question concerning income differences (see table 7.7). However, the party differences are not similar. In this case, the Liberal Party and the Socialist Left Party stand out with the lowest congruence for all the three years studied. This indicates that the differences between parties are related more to the type of issue used in the analysis, and that no party or parties stand out as being particularly unrepresentative at the member level. In this case, the SV voters, along with the Labour voters, are more inclined than the party members to say that we should accept bigger income differences. For the Conservatives and the Progress Party, it is the other way around; party members are more inclined to agree with the statement than the voters.

Table 7.7. Congruence between voters and members after party affiliation/choice. Accept bigger income differences[a]

	1990s			2000s			2010s		
	DM	CoA	AI	DM	CoA	AI	DM	CoA	AI
SV	0.6	67	65	0.6	75	62	0.5	69	73
Ap	0.3	75	80	0.3	81	75	0.3	74	81
Sp	0.1	79	81	0.0	88	89	0.1	70	78
KrF	0.2	78	84	0.0	84	84	0.4	73	81
V	0.8	59	38	0.4	79	80	0.4	79	70
H	0.3	85	75	0.4	72	66	0.1	79	82
FrP	0.3	85	84	0.6	76	71	0.3	81	81
Average	0.2	75	72	0.3	79	75	0.2	75	78

a. Q: To exhort people to greater effort, we should be willing to accept bigger differences in wage levels.

To sum up: These two congruence analyses using identical questions do not indicate that the parties represent voters to a less extent today than they did twenty years ago. Rather, the conclusion is that congruence between voters and members, as a whole and by party, has been stable at what must be characterized as a very high level for the whole period studied.

A Closer Look at Issue Congruence Today

So far, the main focus has been on developments over time. In this last empirical section of the chapter, we study party representation in more detail. The rich data from 2010 enable us to take a more comprehensive look at congruence and policy representation. Seven identical questions were asked to voters, party members, party delegates, and MPs. These seven questions are all related to the central and essential issue dimension in Norwegian politics: taxation, immigration, introduction of gas power plants, foreign aid, environmental protection, gender equality, and the role of labor organizations. Norwegian electoral politics is, as accounted for in chapter 3, multidimensional, and this range of questions enables us to study congruence on several of the most important dimensions.

An analysis on issue congruence today will also tell us something about the level of congruence over time. If congruence is very high today, it cannot have decreased significantly over time. As in the previous two analyses, we begin by studying issue congruence for the totality of voters, members, delegates, and MPs. Figure 7.4 reports the CoAr index for the seven issue dimensions.

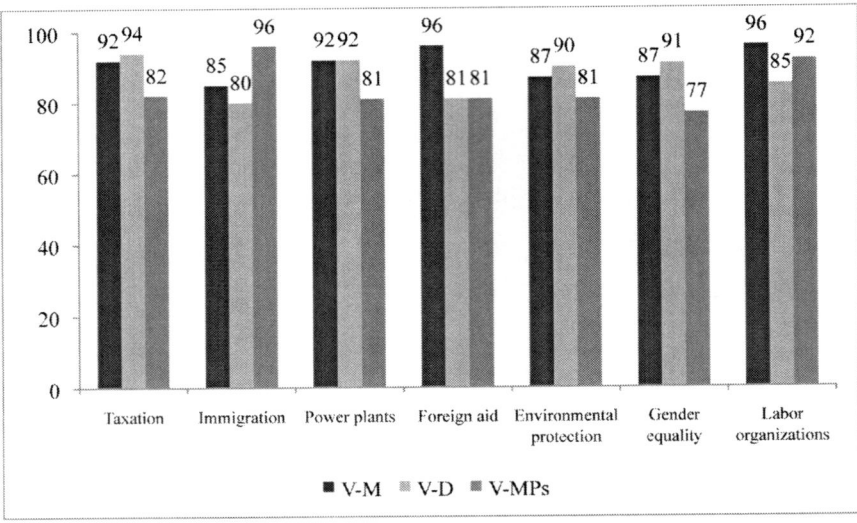

Figure 7.4.   Issue congruence on seven issues 2010. The electorate, all members, delegates, and MPs. CoAr index.[11]

The figure confirms two main patterns that we have seen in the previous analyses. First, the level of congruence must be characterized as very good. The CoAr index for voters and members varies from 80 to 96. Congruence between voters and MPs varies between 77 (gender equality) and 92 (labor organizations).[12] Second, congruence is highest between voters and members and lowest for voters and MPs. The exception to the rule is that on the immigration issue, the agreement between the whole of the electorate and the whole of the parliament is exceptionally good.[13] As the congruence is so good, there are no big differences between voters, members, delegates, and MPs. However, voters, members, and delegates are more inclined to agree that high incomes should be taxed harder. Voters and MPs tend to be more skeptical toward immigration than members and delegates. MPs are more inclined than voters, members, and delegates to agree that gas power plants should be built in Norway. Members, MPs, especially delegates, are more inclined to agree that foreign aid should increase, while voters are more inclined to say that we need more environmental protection. Voters also want more gender equality than members, delegates, and MPs.

Now, we turn to congruence by party. Table 7.8 shows policy congruence on the same seven issue dimensions. The analysis by party supports the tendencies already reported. First, congruence, especially between voters and members, is very good. In more than 80 percent of the cases (35/42), the score is above 80. Second, on average, the pattern supports the earlier findings that congruence decreases at higher levels of party hierarchy. As figure 7.5 shows, the average congruence between voters and members is 86, for voters and delegates it is 77, and the score for voters and MPs is 67. In just four of the 42 cases we study here, congruence is higher for voters and

MPs than for voters and members. For seven of the cases, the score is higher for voters and delegates. While congruence between voters and members scored above 80 in more than 80 percent of the cases, the score was above 80 in ten cases for voters and MPs, and 17 times for voters and delegates.

Table 7.8.　Issue congruence on seven issue dimensions in 2010 by party. CoAr index[a]

	Tax			Immigration			Gas Power Plants		
	M-V	V-D	V-MPs	M-V	V-D	V-MPs	M-V	V-D	V-MPs
SV	84	75	47	91	87	84	93	79	75
Ap	92	86	85	88	69	75	88	87	91
Sp	81	74	63	80	73	52	89	81	56
KrF	95	76	64	64	69	74	91	67	35
V	89	67	n.a.	90	64	n.a.	85	66	n.a.
H	85	77	90	77	86	66	88	78	72
FrP	84	58	57	79	88	78	85	71	53
Average	87	73	68	81	77	72	88	76	64

	Foreign Aid			Environment			Gender Equality		
	M-V	V-D	V-MPs	M-V	V-D	V-MPs	M-V	V-D	V-MPs
SV	93	85	48	95	95	90	97	81	67
Ap	95	77	74	85	89	66	91	92	95
Sp	78	66	58	91	84	86	81	92	87
KrF	81	78	40	74	82	83	81	81	68
V	88	76	n.a.	84	88	n.a.	87	78	n.a.
H	89	85	54	84	79	62	88	74	62
FrP	88	78	84	83	56	44	79	54	32
Average	87	78	60	85	82	72	86	79	69

	Labour Organizations		
	M-V	V-D	V-MPs
SV	93	86	65
Ap	85	59	57
Sp	90	77	55
KrF	80	77	57
V	79	74	n.a.
H	82	73	63
FrP	93	88	75
Average	86	76	62

[a.] See notes to figure 7.4 for question wording.

Some of the scores for the voter-MP relationship are really low. In most cases, the Agree index is low as well, implying that congruence is low in these cases. In most cases, the low score is related to the homogeneity among the party MPs. For example, all representatives from the Socialist Left Party agree completely with the statement that high incomes should be taxed harder (75 percent of SV voters agree completely or somewhat), and 100 percent of KrF-representatives agree completely that foreign aid should increase (70 percent of KrF-voters agree completely or somewhat). In some cases, the MPs and voters just do not agree on issues. This is the case for FrP related to environmental issues and gender equality. For FrP, the Agree index for voters and MPs is three for environmental issues and seven for gender equality.

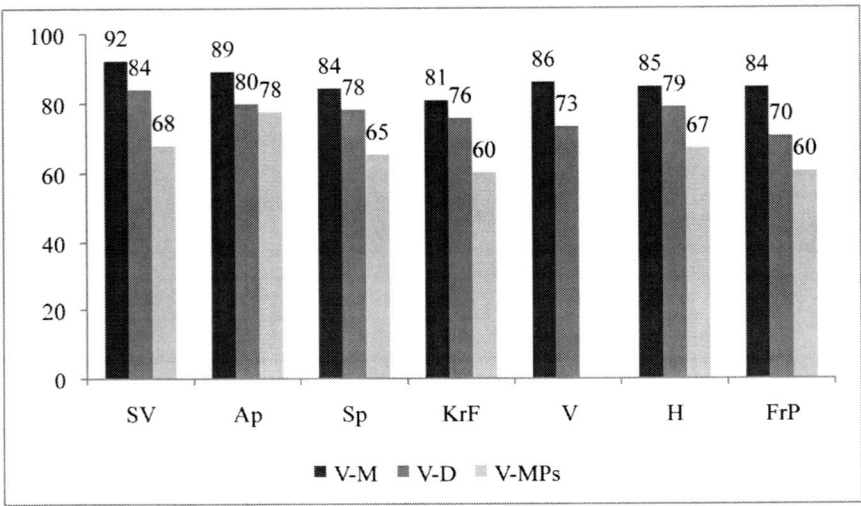

Figure 7.5. Average congruence on seven items in 2010 (2009, 2012). CoAr index.[14]

There are only small differences between the parties. As a rule, all the parties have a high score for all the years and for all three relationships. It varies which party has the highest score from item to item, but there seems to be no specific pattern. It should be noted that the pattern of decreasing congruence higher up in the party hierarchy is more distinct in this analysis, which adds up the party differences than in the analysis of the whole party sphere presented in figure 7.4. We will return to this difference in the discussion below.

DISCUSSION AND CONCLUSION

There is little in our results that suggest that the representative capacity of parties in terms of policy congruence has been reduced in the last decades. Issue congruence between voters and members and voters and delegates has not decreased over the last decades, and neither has issue congruence between voters and MPs. As a rule, the congruence between voters and MPs was lower than the congruence between voters and members. Let us sum up and discuss the results in more detail.

The first research question we addressed was about the parties' ability to channel preferences through the party organization. Has the congruence between voters and members and voters and delegates decreased over time? The short answer to this question is no. Issue congruence is high for the whole period, and although there are fluctuations, there is no clear trend toward either increasing or decreasing congruence. This is particularly evident in the longitudinal analysis of voters and members where we used two identical questions for all three points in time. Both the analysis for the whole of the party sphere and the analysis by party showed the same tendency: stability on a relatively high congruence level.

The second part of the research question asked if congruence between voters and MPs had decreased over time. Although the data are less adequate for voters and MPs, the short answer to this question is also no. The results indicate that congruence between voters and MPs, for the party sphere as a whole and for the individual parties, has been stable at a high level. It should also be noted that congruence between voters and members was, as a rule, higher than the congruence between voters and delegates, and in particular, higher than congruence between voters and MPs. This relationship is valid for the whole period covered, but is more distinct in the party analysis than in the analysis for the whole party sphere. Our study supports the notion that polarization and internal agreement increases higher up in the party hierarchy (see chapter 2). All the MPs combined, consisting of party groups with differing views, constitute a more diverse group, leading to better congruence in the total analyses. We will return to this issue in chapter 8.

With regard to the differences among parties, we found no support for the hypothesis that parties with a particularly steep membership decline experienced a steeper decline in congruence compared to other parties. Rather, congruence differed among parties in a somewhat unsystematic way. This applies to voters and members, voters and delegates, as well as between voters and MPs. The findings in some earlier congruence studies that the parties on the right, as a rule, have lower congruence than parties on the left (Holmberg 2000), was not evident in our material. No party stood out as a party with particularly good or bad congruence among parties.

In some of the smaller parties, there could be a methodological explanation for fluctuations. If all nine MPs place themselves in the middle category—as the Centre Party representative did on the Christian values question in 2005—congruence will necessarily be low. For the parliament as a whole, the number of MPs is higher, and the distribution of preferences will be more evenly distributed, consequently increasing congruence for the overall party sphere. There are limits as to how congruent party voters and representatives can be expected to be. It should be noted that although all parties scored above 80 on congruence between voters and members (CoAr index) in 2010, the Socialist Left Party scored particularly high.

The most important result from the congruence analysis by party is that when we consider the totality of issues, the voters, members, delegates, and representatives from one party have clear congruent profiles that differentiate them from the other party profiles. This shows that voters have a choice, and are well represented by the parties they choose. That said, it is important to remember that we have used issues that are all deeply rooted in the national cleavage structure, key issues related not only to the economic left-right axis, but also to newer conflict dimensions like economic growth vs. environment protection. These issues are important to all the parties examined; they are often intensely debated in electoral campaigns and have been important for people's party choice on Election Day (e.g., Karlsen and Aardal 2011). We do not know whether issue congruence also holds for more minor issues, or issues that are not firmly rooted in the general cleavage structure.

Then again, we know that issues that are less salient or connected are often also less consequential and are, therefore, less important for political representation. As argued, we cannot expect voters to have clear opinions in all kinds of issues, and we cannot expect parties to mirror the voters' opinion to the same extent in non-salient, more specific policy questions without roots in the national pattern of cleavages and issue dimensions. To conclude, congruence between voters and members and voters and delegates has been on a relatively high level for the whole period covered. This indicates that parties still channel policy preferences through their organization, and that the party organization may be an essential aspect of party representation. In the next chapter, we will discuss this issue further and consider the evidence presented in this chapter, as well as in chapters 4, 5, and 6 in relation to the analytical framework sketched out in chapters 1 and 2.

NOTES

1. As discussed in chapter 2, the notion that MPs are more extreme than voters refers to MPs and voters as groups. A fair amount of voters will be just as "extreme" as their representatives, while others will hold less extreme views or disagree with the majority of the representatives. Hence, rather than extreme, homogeneous is a better term to describe the opinion pattern of MPs.

2. $100-(|Ax-Ay|)+(|DAx-DAy|)$.

3. As a comparison, for SV voters and MPs the CoAr index is 85 and the Agree index is 70.

4. Congruence based on the 2009 elections surveys is lower than the results based on the Gallup data.

5. See the discussion in chapter 4. We weigh delegates based on party members because we consider them representatives of the membership party. To compare the totality of voters with unweighted delegates would not make much sense.

6. To get a grip on the score of the CoAr index and the Agree index, we have compared the voters, members, and MPs of different parties. For the immigration issue in 2010, the CoAr score is 28 and the Agree index is −32 for SV (voters) and FrP (members), and 29 (CoAr) and −25 (AI) for SV (voters) and FrP (MPs). However, Ap and the Conservatives do not differ that

much on this issue as both the CoAr and Agree index is 75 for voters and members. Moreover, the scores for the Ap-H relationship is considerably lower when it comes to reducing taxes on high incomes. The CoAr index is 54 and the Agree index is only 24 for Ap-voters and H-members, and for the relationship between A-voters and H-MPs, the CoAr index is 37 and the Agree index is −21.

7. Congruence between voters and MPs is particularly low for the Centre Party in 2000. This is because all the MPs chose the "neither nor" category, which is hardly used by the voters (see the methodological discussion).

8. Q: It is better to develop public services than to reduce taxation.

The difference in mean has been multiplied by 100 and subtracted from 100. Hence, a score of 100 indicates perfect congruence, no difference in the mean.

9. Q: To exhort people to greater effort, we should be willing to accept bigger differences in wage levels.

The difference in mean has been multiplied by 100 and subtracted from 100. Hence, a score of 100 indicates perfect congruence, no difference in the mean.

10. 46 vs. 7 (1990), 38 vs. 11 (2000), and 52 vs. 16 (2010).

11. Higher incomes should be taxed harder than they are today.

Immigration is a serious threat to our national identity.

We should develop gas-power plants in Norway even though CO_2 cleaning will not be possible with today's technology.

We should increase transfers to developing countries.

We should focus more on environmental protection even if it means lower personal consumption.

One should pave the way to bring more equality between women and men.

The large organizations in business and industry has too much power in today's society.

12. The third main pattern in the previous analyses, stable congruence, is not studied here.

13. Taxes, immigration, and power plants are also reported in table 7.1. In this analysis, we use the Gallup data. As mentioned in this survey, the middle category was presented to the respondents, and the congruence scores are higher in these analyses than in the ones we have presented above using the national elections surveys.

14. See figure 7.4 for the question wording of the seven items.

8

Representative Capacity after the Mass Party

Political parties play a key role in representative democracies: democracies are even "unthinkable" without them. Nonetheless, parties change, often in fundamental ways. What happens to their positions in democracy? This book has addressed the issue of whether declining membership and increased dependency on public finance has made political parties less able to represent voters, as is claimed in much of the current scholarly literature. In our view, we cannot take for granted that declining membership in parties will by default lead to less representative parties. This is not least because the mechanisms for representation are not only embedded in party organizations, but can also be found in the arena of competitive elections.

Although our point of departure has been the renewed debate on party changes after the golden era of the "mass parties," where Katz and Mair's new model of a "cartel party" is a focal point, we have not designed our study as a test of the cartel thesis. This thesis is much broader than the elements we have focused on here. Still it is fair to say that membership decline and increase of public finance are important and perhaps the most well-documented aspects of mass party decline—and key factors in the discussion of whether parties' representative capacity has changed as well.

In the book we have shown that the existing empirical studies are not able to substantiate the claims of decline in parties' ability to provide representation, but above all that in Norway, decline of mass parties has not led to a decrease in the representative capacity of party organizations in terms of intra-party activity and social and political congruence. Party members and elites, as well as the parties' MPs, still represent voters fairly well. Why this "negative" result? We cannot know for sure without more comprehensive comparative and longitudinal studies. In this chapter we speculate on the importance—at least for the Norwegian case—of a few factors earlier singled out for special consideration (cf. chapter 2). First we briefly consider the possible threshold mechanism that indicates a "sufficient" level of membership (as discussed in chapter 1). Then we look at three factors that appear most relevant in this single-country study: 1) the development of party competition for votes, 2) stability and change in the system for candidate/MP selection, and 3) the formal organizational structures of parties outside public office.

In the last section, we consider possible general lessons that may be drawn from this study of mass party decline, and the role of party organizations in contemporary democracies. We argue that the documented party changes are more likely to result in reduced representative capacity if the formal organizational structures of the original mass parties are also transformed. First, however, we summarize the empirical findings of both the "meta-study" presented in chapter 3 and the longitudinal case study of Norway in chapters 4–7 in some detail.

ANALYZING PREVIOUS RESEARCH: WHAT DID WE FIND?

The review of previous studies in chapter 3 indicated that there are fairly stable levels of activity among party members over time, and that internal party democracy probably has weakened due to changing conditions: in particular the impact of the media. In discussing social representativeness, a few studies have reported an increased social gap between members and voters. Party MPs, on the other hand, seem to have become more exclusive in most regards, with one exception: gender. The representation of men and women has become somewhat more equal. Most importantly, the difference in self-placement along the left-right axis between voters and the party levels does not appear to have changed. Overall, the limited empirical evidence that exists provides few indications of a decline in representative capacities for party organizations. We also find no trace of a widening gap in political representation for the MPs during this period. This is in contrast to the rather strong claims that have been made that such gaps are to be expected, since parties appear to have drifted away from their anchorages in civil society.

The studies of the descriptive and substantive representativeness of MPs, however, rarely link their findings to (or even include) possible changes among party members and activists. The exception is Rohrschneider and Whitefield's (2012) study on Eastern and Western Europe concluding that, what they label, the "mass parties" of the West are still critical in providing voter–party congruence. We still maintain that the alleged decline in party organizations as agencies of representation has neither been confirmed nor rejected by empirical studies. Such studies would indeed be difficult to undertake, since longitudinal data on party members and activists barely exist, or are rather impressionistic if they do exist. The existing comparative empirical analyses simply have not addressed the effects of declining membership on the policies of parties within democratic institutions.

THE CASE STUDY OF NORWAY: STABILITY AND CHANGE

In the case study of Norwegian parties presented in chapters 4–7, we were able to analyze such longitudinal data across party strata. We documented that party membership has fallen by nearly half since the 1980s, and public party support has increased tremendously during that time. Based on a broad set of survey data on voters, members, delegates, and MPs from the last two decades, we have mapped changes in patterns of activity and influence, and in social and political congruence, along various issue dimensions, across party strata, and over time.

Activity

We found no trace of party members becoming less active between 1991 and 2009. Although participation was reported to be low, the share of party members who participated in different activities actually increased slightly during that period. The members also contacted their representatives in public office just as often in 2009 as they did in 1991. An increasing share of the membership was also under the impression that the leadership was paying attention to the members. No evidence supported the claim that those parties that were losing the most members were more exposed to declining activism and decreased bottom-up influence than parties with stable or rising memberships.[1] In other words, the expectation that members' activities and influence had declined was not supported in our study.

This result suggests that, in terms of activity, some of the assumptions that are fundamental to the party decline literature might be unrealistic: first, that those who leave the parties are as engaged as those who stay behind, and second, that the remaining members are inevitably marginalized due to their low numbers and decreasing importance to the party. If decline in membership means that the least engaged members leave the party, this will automatically raise the relative activity levels inside the parties. In our view, the decline in membership has given a stronger presence to the remaining "quality members": namely, people who have stronger political interest, and those who have available time or who are willing to prioritize party work. That said, the overall presence of active party members in Norwegian politics has declined as the total number of members has gone down.

Social Representativeness

The next question we asked was whether the social congruence between voters and party members, delegates, and MPs has changed. The study reaffirmed Scarrow and Gezgor's (2010) study of European party members, and found no clear trend toward weakened congruence across party levels. We did, however, find that the party members had become somewhat older and better educated than the voters. The MPs today are less similar to voters than they used to be in terms of education, occupation, and sector affiliation. People with higher education, those working as senior white-collar employees, and those employed in the public sector or by organizations (such as political parties), have all become more overrepresented in the Norwegian Parliament. Yet the link *between* these "negative developments" does not seem to be a strong one. Weakened voter–member age congruence has not led to the recruitment of older, mid-level party elites or MPs, as we discuss in more detail below. We find that Putman's "law of increasing disproportion" applies: the more selective the group of politicians, the larger the background differences compared to ordinary voters. Weakened socio-economic congruence at higher party levels, however, does not seem to be driven by changes in party membership—with the partial exception of education. When looking at the parties whose membership is in decline, we find no trend that these parties have also declined in social congruence, while the other parties have not.

Norwegian party members have not changed into "the outer ring of an extended political class" (van Biezen, Mair, and Poguntke 2012). Overall, the changes in members' profiles have been limited, and many of these changes match the general social developments that have also affected voters (such as the decrease in number of blue-collar workers and increase in level of education). The relative stability in voter-member social congruence thus seems to originate both in the limited changes in recruitment patterns and in the parallel changes among the voters. The weaker voter–member age congruence has not spread to the level of party congress delegates or to the candidates/MPs. In terms of demography, today the parties' grassroots members are less like voters than the higher-strata party members, although the gender congruence is better among delegates than it is among MPs. We did find weakened socio-economic congruence at higher party levels, but—with the notable exception of education—this result did not seem to be driven by changes in the members' profiles. Party members have not become much different in terms of occupation, for example. It would appear that what happens at the membership level is of limited importance for the selection of mid-level elites and candidates for public office.

Policy Representativeness

The most important question, however, is whether or not there is a weakening in policy congruence between voters and the different party strata. The short answer, in light of the chapter 7 results, is no. Although there are fluctuations, the congruence between voters, members, and delegates remains high over the entire period, and across issue dimensions like economy, morality/immigration, and environmental issues. Congruence is also high between the voters and the MPs. This applies both when looking at the overall party-voter congruence and that of the parties individually. There is no clear trend toward either increasing or decreasing congruence. Again, we find no support for the expectation that parties with high membership decline had lower (or decreasing) congruence compared to parties with stable membership. Congruence levels seemed to differ between parties in a fairly unsystematic way.

We observed that congruence between voters and members was, as a rule, higher than the congruence between voters and delegates and, in particular, the congruence between voters and MPs—especially in the analyses of individual parties. One explanation for this is that internal agreement (and party discipline) increases the higher in the party hierarchy one gets. The parties' MPs are homogeneous in their expressed beliefs on most issues; they echo the party's programmatic policies on the issue, even when opinions of party voters are more diverse. The grassroots members within the party organizations, on the other hand, are able to include more of the variation that is also found at the voter level. All of the MPs combined (consisting of party groups with differing views) constitute a more heterogeneous group, however, which leads to better congruence at the aggregate level.

Ideally, we could have tested the hypotheses on a broader range of policy issues than we did. What would the result have been if we had also included issues without solid roots in the cleavage structure? Still, we will argue that the stability and relatively high level of congruence on essentially all issues is remarkable. We have found that Norwegian party members, delegates, and MPs have not become more detached from their voters since the 1990s, as far as major political conflict dimensions are concerned; quite to the contrary. We thus may conclude that "mass party decline" has not been able to move parties—members, delegates, and MPs—away from the voters in terms of major policy issues. Nor are there any notable differences between the old (declining) parties or the new (more stable) parties on these scores.

EXPLAINING THE RELATIVE STABILITY IN PARTIES' REPRESENTATIVE CAPACITIES

Taken together, the results tell us that decreasing membership and increased state financing of parties do not necessarily lead to party organizations losing out on their representative capacity. One reason why the data did not support this widely held hypothesis could be that there is a threshold effect involved: that the decrease must reach a "tipping point" in order to take effect.[2] Young (2013, 75–76) wonders whether even today's small membership in some parties could be "sufficient to make parties appear connected to the electorate and attentive to democratic norms in their internal operation." In other words, *democratic legitimacy* for membership parties may only require a low level of membership. As for providing *representative capacity* to supplement the election arena, however, the demands may be higher. Perhaps Norwegian party organizations are not sufficiently weakened (and haven't lost enough members) to lose their capacity to represent? Yet it is not obvious where such a threshold would lie. In addition, is it the number of members or a certain proportion of the electorate that will be the crucial factor? In any case, such a potential threshold effect can only be found through longitudinal studies across countries.

Another major question is whether the political congruence between voters and MPs is due to happenings *within party organizations* or if it reflects that elites are *adapting to the external competition for votes*. If party members and delegates over time became less congruent with the voters' policy views, but the congruence between voters and MPs remained high, this would indicate that party organizations' importance for channeling preferences from voters to parliament had declined. The crucial mechanism for party representation would in that case be the elections, guiding the parties and their MPs toward voter congruence. Our empirical analyses have demonstrated, however, that Norwegian party elites are faced with members and delegates that do not distort voter opinions (as would be expected on the basis of May's law). Indeed, the congruence between voters and members was, as a rule, higher than between voters and MPs.

Of course, this is not to say that party competition does not matter. On the whole, as we argued in chapter 4, parties still compete for votes with relative efficiency and provide voters with alternative policy packages on election day. In this way, the relationship *between* parties certainly does continue to contribute to the parties' relatively stable representative capacity in Parliament. In this book, however, we have concentrated on what happens within and around the party membership organizations: namely, the system for candidate/MP selection and the development of party membership organizations as formal structures.

Candidate Selection and Party Discipline

Norwegian parties still nominate fairly representative MPs for elections, also in cases where members have become somewhat less like voters socially. This could mean that the fundamental causes for party representation are external. For example, increased gender equality in society at large certainly means that more women run for office and contribute to gender balance among mid-level elites, as well as in party lists. It is important to acknowledge, however, that such changes happen by means of parties' own selection of congressional delegates and candidates for public office, and not as a direct result of greater cultural developments.

The candidate selection process for the party lists is the result of closed party conventions at the county level (cf. chapter 4). In this way, the Norwegian election system opens up for ticket balancing by parties, a feature that might positively affect the social and political representativeness of MPs. By providing gender balance, for instance, a party might hope to attract more voters. As such, by looking more closely at the data, party decision-makers—and their selection criteria—might well be the key here. The party selectorates seem to counteract skewed members' output by recruiting delegates and list candidates that are *demographically* closer to the electorate than the regular members. The selectorates do, however, select mid-level elites and politicians that are less similar to voters in terms of their *socio-economic* background. Despite the general stability revealed, various parties have used their control over candidate selection to both *strengthen* (e.g., gender) and *weaken* (e.g., education) the social congruence of MPs, and not by simply mirroring the membership profile. In addition, as mentioned in chapter 4 and as we will elaborate below, the party-controlled candidate selection process still nurtures a high level of party discipline in the legislature. Hence, party MPs continue to be kept in line with the party program, despite weakened socio-economic congruence.

Thus, what happens within the party organizations during candidate selection, the election system, and the stimuli offered by party competition for votes seem to intertwine, in particular as far as the social representativeness of MPs goes.

FORMAL ORGANIZATIONAL STRUCTURE OF PARTY ORGANIZATIONS

Although we have no real empirical evidence for the decline in the representative capacity of party organizations in other countries, we will nevertheless suggest that Norwegian parties have certain qualities that might hamper the potential negative effects of membership decline. Rohrschneider and Whitefield, comparing the parties of Eastern Europe with those of the West, still labelled parties in Western Europe "mass parties." However, we also know that there is variation in organizational structures among parties in old democracies today. In the last thirty years, parties around the world have not only lost members; many parties have also experienced substantial organizational reforms in the direction of direct democracy (Pilet and Cross 2014; Scarrow 2015). Reforms have been related to the selection of party leaders, policy-making processes, and candidate selection. The introduction of membership ballots has, according to several scholars (e.g., Poguntke and Webb 2005), led to a strengthening of party leadership at the expense of party activists. This claim echoes Duverger, who argued that the representative intra-party democracy is the *most distinctive* feature of the mass party, although mass membership and finance obviously are important as well. Yet, not all former "mass parties" have gone through a wholesale organizational transformation. Hence, it is worth noting that as a rule, Norwegian parties have reacted to membership decline by organizational maintenance, rather than through reform (Allern and Karlsen 2014a).

Norwegian parties still clearly bear the structural characteristics of the typical mass party: policy manifestos are approved of by the party congress, and party leaders are elected by representative party organs and held accountable to party members and activists. In addition, parties' mid-level activists—at the regional level—still control the candidate selection process. The question is if this organizational stability—the survival of the formal organizational structure of the mass party—has acted as a countervailing force to representative decline in Norway. Within the organizational structure of mass parties, accountability is built into the party organization. As a result, members have influence in the party, and this most likely contributes to party programs that mostly reflect the opinions of members. MPs risk not being re-nominated if party members and delegates are unhappy with how they follow up on the party manifesto. Given that members and activists have not become distinct political elites, but reflect the voters in both descriptive and political terms, these organizational structures most likely play a part in making party-based representation work. A few studies have indicated that decentralized and inclusive candidate selection methods are likely to produce less representative candidate lists in terms of background (Rahat, Hazan, and Katz 2008; Hazan and Rahat 2010).

Formal organizational structure thus could be an essential factor in understanding the representative capacity of parties. In Norway, extensive party programs, strong formal party organizations with representative democracy, including candidate selection by mid-level activists, contribute to control of party elites and high parliamentary group discipline. As noted in chapter 4, the party manifesto is regarded as binding for party representatives in public office at all levels.

A Special Norwegian Context?

Finally, we need to consider two contextual features that might make Norwegian parties particularly resistant to change. First, the affluence that comes with Norway's considerable oil revenues makes the pressure for welfare retrenchment less likely than in other, less fortunate countries. Fewer financial constraints make it easier for Norwegian party elites to accommodate voter and member grievances than for party elites elsewhere in the world. That said, some have argued that with the establishment of the Norwegian oil fund, the level of support for incumbent parties has regularly eroded. Dissatisfaction with government policies has turned the oil wealth into a form of "resource curse" for Norwegian governments, making it difficult for parties to win two elections in a row. This has happened even in prosperous times when there has been increased public spending (Listhaug and Narud 2011).

Another possible counter-force is cultural. No doubt Norway is a small country, with an egalitarian political culture, a relatively high level of political trust, and strong norms of participatory democracy. As a result, in normative terms, the mainstream media as well as the government still expect parties to work as "schools of democracy" through party activism and intra-party democracy. These cultural aspects might temper the professionalization of political parties. Parties still strive to recruit new members from different segments; and, even if party members and activists become less like the average voter, parties use the "ticket-balancing" selection of candidates for public office to make parties appear representative before elections (Heidar and Saglie 2002). Only comparative research can tell whether or not such factors actually matter.

REPRESENTATIVE DEMOCRACY AFTER THE MASS PARTY

In this book, we have discussed how political parties operate and connect citizens and the state after the demise of traditional mass parties. Focusing on representation through party members, delegates, and MPs, we have not found very much empirical support in relevant current empirical studies; nor have we found support for the proposition that parties' representative capacity has declined in Norway. Norwegian parties have continued to be representative, despite significant party membership decline and increased party dependence on state subventions. As most of the possible explanations we have discussed are not unique to the Norwegian case, we have reason to believe that party organizations' persistent capacity to represent voters could apply to other countries as well, in spite of the decline of such parties as mass membership organizations.

We have argued that parties' abilities to represent voters could be the result of the party organization, the competition for votes, or both. The analyses support the claim that party organizations still have representative capacity. In addition, there seems to be interplay between organizational factors and the stimuli that are offered by party competition for votes. The persistent and high congruence between voters and MPs fits well with the general research that has been conducted on party competition based on manifesto data. Numerous tests of programmatic convergence have been negative (e.g., Laver and Budge 1992) or only partly supportive of the thesis (Volkens and Klingemann 2002; Budge, Pennings, and Keman 2012). As Enyedi (2014, 198) points out, the threat of newcomers and the fundamental logic of multiparty competition are able to prevent convergence. The work to maintain the voter-party linkage could also find additional help from monitoring agencies, vigorous media action, and courts than before; better-educated voters make it more difficult for party elites to collude and to drift away from the voters (Enyedi 2014, 199). We found in chapter 7 that all seven Norwegian parties emerged as being distinctively different in terms of aggregated policy views. Thus, the voters do have a choice, and appear to be well represented by these parties.

At the same time, we suggest that Norway's closed party-controlled candidate selection processes, and the survival of the mass party's formal representative structures, could make Norwegian parties relatively resistant to representative decline. If not fighting for the party program, the MPs and the party leadership risk facing a disgruntled party organization that has the power to remove them from office. The formal intra-party democracy in Norway seems to strengthen voter-MP congruence rather than to detract from it, which is probably aided by Norway's strong egalitarian and participatory political culture.

In future analyses one should bear in mind that the social congruence and policy congruence between voters and MPs may be affected both by party organizations and by electoral competition. This is a lesson of relevance for the party literature on "declining mass parties," as well as for voter-delegate representation studies—albeit for opposite reasons. Whereas studies in the former tend to ignore the potential of the electoral channel, the latter studies tend to overlook parties as organizations. One reasonable hypothesis is that competition for votes produces congruence in a limited number of issues, but will not secure congruence along a wider range of policy fields. We wonder also if pure electoral parties will be able to create the same level of social congruence, even if parties balance tickets in order to appeal to a wider range of voters. The party organizations will likely create a more varied pool of potential candidates for public office by operating "schools of democracy and politics."

As we noted in chapter 2, there is a notable difference in the post-war literature on parties between alternative normative ideals. This reflected in general also a divide between US and European scholars. At the core of the debate was the importance of electoral competition versus membership organization. Schematically speaking, parties in US politics were concerned with giving voters an electoral choice: they presented fairly independent candidates fighting for votes under a common label, and offered the voters the opportunity to hold their representatives accountable. The party organization, its membership, and the party activists did not have important parts in this system—or they played an outright negative role in terms of producing less representative candidates. Consequently, if the party organizations withered— what is the problem?

The European countries, on the other hand, had a tradition of strong party organizations: the parties had numerous active members, and the party organizations produced policies and programs that carried strong weight with the MPs. Party representatives acted in a highly unitary fashion within institutions, on the basis of the party program. Internal party democracy, with members and activists debating policies on the basis of a common interest—an "ideology"—was seen as a prerequisite for national democracy. National democracy was normatively based on internally democratic parties. This was the premise of the "mass party" as described by (among others) Maurice Duverger. The decline of the mass party, including the weakened party membership and the rise and increase of public party finance, also threatened the role of parties as representative institutions.

This idealized description of the mass party, however, might have led to exaggerated descriptions of membership decline, as suggested by Scarrow (2015). No doubt fewer and less active party members weaken and limit parties' abilities to promote participatory norms of democracy. But whether it also means a weakened representative capacity of party organizations—as reflected in individual characteristics and policy programs, all the way to public office—is another question.

Future research will have to deal more explicitly with the various possible drivers of parties' representative capacity as organizations since this will require a comparative approach. In this book we have shown that parties can continue to represent, even "after the mass party."

NOTES

1. As parties' dependency on state financing did not vary significantly, we did not expect any differences according to variation in membership finances.
2. Malcolm Gladwell's famous phrase (Young 2013, 75).

Bibliography

Aardal, Bernt. 2003. *Velgere i villrede.* Oslo: Damm & Søn.

———, ed. 2011. *Det politiske landskap. En studie av stortingsvalget i 2009.* Oslo: Cappelen-Damm.

———. 2015. "Politiske verdier og stemmegivning. " In *Valg og velgere. En studie av stortings-valget 2013*, edited by Bernt Aardal and Johannes Bergh, 34–48. Oslo: Cappelen-Damm.

Aldrich, John H. 2011. *Why Parties? A Second Look.* Chicago: The University of Chicago Press.

Allern, Elin H. 2010a. "Parties as Vehicles of Democracy in Norway: Still Working after All These Years?" In *Europe.* Vol. 2 of *Political Parties and Democracy,* edited by Kay Lawson, 139–58. Westport, Conn.: Praeger.

———. 2010b. *Political Parties and Interest Groups in Norway.* Colchester: ECPR Press.

———. 2010c. "The Survival of a Majority Coalition: The Norwegian 2009 Parliamentary Elections," *West European Politics* 33: 904–12.

Allern, Elin H., and Rune Karlsen. 2014a. "Unanimous, by Acclamation? Party Leader Selection in Norway." In *The Selection of Party Leaders in Parliamentary Systems,* edited by Jean-Benoit Pilet and William Cross, 47–61. London: Palgrave.

———. 2014b. "A Turn to the Right: The Norwegian Parliamentary Election of September 9 2013." *West European Politics* 37:653–63.

Allern, Elin H., Rune Karlsen, and Hanne Marthe Narud. 2014. "Stortingets sosiale sam-mensetning." In *Stortingets historie 1964–2014,* edited by Hanne Marthe Narud, Knut Heidar, and Tore Grønlie. Bergen: Fagbokforlaget.

Allern, Elin H., and Karina Pedersen. 2007. "The Impact of Party Organizational Changes on Democracy." *West European Politics* 30:69–92.

Allern, Elin H., and Jo Saglie. 2012. "Inside the Black Box: Parties as Multi-level Organiza-tions in a Unitary State." *West European Politics* 35:947–70.

Almond, Gabriel A. 1960. "A Functional Approach to Comparative Politics." In *The Politics of Developing Areas,* edited by Gabriel A. Almond and James S. Coleman. Princeton, NJ: Princeton University Press.

Andeweg, Rudy B. 2011. "Approaching Perfect Policy Congruence: Measurement, Development, and Relevance for Political Representation." In *How Democracy Works: Political Representation and Policy Congruence in Modern Societies*, edited by Bas Denters, Martin Rosema, and Kees Aarts, 39–52. Amsterdam: Amsterdam University Press.

Assarson, Jan. 1993. "Bör partierna vara internt demokratiska? En studie i ett normativt och begreppsligt problem." *Statsvetenskaplig Tidskrift* 96:39–68.

Aylott, Nicholas. Forthcoming. "Parties and Party Systems in the North." In *Democratic Institutions in Decline?* edited by Torbjörn Bergman and Kaare Strøm. Ann Arbor: University of Michigan Press.

Bäck, Mats, and Tommy Möller. 1997. *Partier och organisationer*. Stockholm: Norstedts Juridik AB.

Bagehot, Walter. (1867) 2002. *The English Constitution*. Oxford: Oxford University Press. First published by Chapman and Hall.

Barnes, Samuel H. 1976. *Representation in Italy: Institutionalized Tradition and Electoral Change*. Chicago: Chicago University Press.

Bartolini, Stefano, and Peter Mair. 2001. "Challenges to Contemporary Parties." In *Political Parties and Democracy*, edited by Larry Diamond and Richard Gunther, 327–43. Baltimore: The Johns Hopkins University Press.

Belchior, Ana Maria. 2013. "Explaining Left–Right Party Congruence Across European Party Systems: A Test of Micro-, Meso-, and Macro-Level Models." *Comparative Political Studies* 46:352–86.

Belchior, Ana Maria, and André Freire. 2013. "Is Party Type Relevant to an Explanation of Policy Congruence? Catchall versus Ideological Parties in the Portuguese case." *International Political Science Review* 34:273–88.

Bergman, Torbjörn, and Kaare Strøm, eds. 2011. *The Madisonian Turn. Political Parties and Parliamentary Democracy in Nordic Countries*. Ann Arbor: The University of Michigan Press.

Best, Heinrich. 2007. "New Challenges, New Elites? Changes in the Recruitment and Career Patterns of European Representative Elites." *Comparative Sociology* 6:85–113.

Best, Heinrich, and Maurizio Cotta. 2000. "Elite Transformation and Modes of Representation since the Mid-Nineteenth Century: Some Theoretical Considerations." In *Parliamentary Representatives in Europe 1848–2000*, edited by Heinrich Best and Maurizio Cotta, 1–28. Oxford: Oxford University Press.

van Biezen, Ingrid. 2004a. "How Political Parties Shape Democracy." CSD Working Paper 04–16, Center for the Study of Democracy, University of California, Irvine. http://reposi tories.cdlib.org/csd/04–16.

———. 2004b. "Political Parties as Public Utilities." *Party Politics* 10:701–22.

van Biezen, Ingrid. 2011. "Constitutionalizing Party Democracy: The Constitutive Codification of Political Parties in Post-war Europe." *British Journal of Political Science* 42:187–212.

van Biezen, Ingrid, Peter Mair, and Thomas Poguntke. 2012. "Going, going, . . . gone? The decline of party membership in contemporary Europe." *European Journal of Political Research* 51:24–56.

van Biezen, Ingrid, and Thomas Poguntke. 2014. "The Decline of Membership-Based Politics." *Party Politics* 20:205–16.

Bryce, James. 1921. *Modern Democracies*. 2 vols. New York: Macmillan.

Buch Jensen, Roger. 1999. "Opinion Structures in Political Parties—The Law of Increasing Polarization?" In *Elites, Parties and Democracy. Festschrift for Professor Mogens N. Pedersen*, edited by Erik Beukel, Kurt Klaudi Klausen, and Poul Erik Mouritzen. Odense: Odense University Press.

Budge, Ian Michael McDonald, Paul Pennings, and Hans Keman, eds. 2012. *Organizing Democratic Choice: Party Representation over Time.* Oxford: Oxford University Press.

Burke, Edmund. 2014. "Speech to the Electors of Bristol." November 3, 1774. Accessed May 23. http://oll.libertyfund.org/titles/burke-select-works-of-edmund-burke-vol-4.

Childs, Sarah. 2013. "Intra-Party Democracy: A Gendered Critique and a Feminist Agenda." In *The Challenges of Intra-Party Democracy*, edited by William P. Cross and Richard S. Katz, 81–99. Oxford: Oxford University Press.

Converse, Phillipe E., and Roy Pierce. 1986. *Political Representation in France.* Cambridge, MA: Harvard University Press.

Costello, Rory, Jacques Thomassen, and Martin Rosema. 2012. "European Parliament Elections and Political Representation: Policy Congruence between Voters and Parties." *West European Politics* 35:1226–48.

Cox, Gary W., and Mathew D. McCubbins. 1993. *Legislative Leviathan: Party Government in the House.* Berkeley: University of California Press.

Cross, William P., and Richard S. Katz. 2013. "The Challenges of Intra-Party Democracy." In *The Challenges of Intra-Party Democracy*, edited by William P. Cross and Richard S. Katz, 1–10. Oxford: Oxford University Press.

Cross, William, and Lisa Young. 2004. "The Contours of Political Party Membership in Canada." *Party Politics* 10:427–44.

Crotty, William. 2006. "Party Origins and Evolution in the United States." In *Handbook of Party Politics,* edited by Richard S. Katz and William J. Crotty, 25–33. London: Sage.

Dahl, Robert A. 1956. *A Preface to Democratic Theory.* Chicago: University of Chicago Press.

Dalton, Russell J. 1985. "Political Parties and Political Representation: Party Supporters and Party Elites in Nine Nations." *Comparative Political Studies* 18:267–99.

Dalton, Russell J. 2000. "The Decline of Party Identifications." In *Parties without Partisans,* edited by Russell J. Dalton and Martin P. Wattenberg, 19–36. Oxford: Oxford University Press.

Dalton, Russell J. 2006. *Citizen Politics. Public Opinion and Political Parties in Advanced Industrial Democracies.* Washington, DC: CQ Press.

Dalton, Russell J., Ian McAllister, and Martin P. Wattenberg 2000. "The Consequences of Partisan Dealignment." In *Parties without Partisans,* edited by Russell J. Dalton and Martin P. Wattenberg, 37–63. Oxford: Oxford University Press.

Dalton, Russell J., and Martin P. Wattenberg, eds. 2000. *Parties without Partisans.* Oxford: Oxford University Press.

Dalton, Russell J., David Farrell, and Ian McAllister. 2011. *Political Parties & Democratic Linkage: How Parties Organize Democracies.* Oxford: Oxford University Press.

Delhey, Jan, and Kenneth Newton. 2005. "Predicting Cross-National Levels of Social Trust: Global Pattern or Nordic Exceptionalism?" *European Sociological Review* 21:311–27.

Demker, Marie, and Lars Svåsand, eds. 2005. *Partiernas århundrade. Fempartimodellens uppgång och fall i Norge och Sverige.* Stockholm: Santèrus Forlag.

Deschouwer, Kris, ed. 2008. *New Parties in Government: In Power for the First Time.* London: Routledge/ECPR Studies in European Political Science.

Downs, Anthony. 1957. *An Economic Theory of Democracy.* New York: Harper and Row Publishers.

Dryzek, John S. 2000. *Deliberative Democracy and Beyond.* Oxford: Oxford University Press.

Duverger, Maurice. (1954) 1972. *Political Parties: Their Organization and Activity in the Modern State*. London: Methuen.

Eliassen, Kjell, and Marit Sjøvaag Marino. 2000. "Democratization and Parliamentary Elite Recruitment in Norway 1848–1996." In *Parliamentary Representatives in Europe 1848–2000*, edited by Heinrich Best and Maurizio Cotta, 310–40. Oxford: Oxford University Press.

Eliassen, Kjell A., and Kjell Sælen. 1971. *Rekrutteringen til den parlamentariske elite i Norge 1814–1970*. Dataarkivene, Department of Sociology, University of Bergen.

Enyedi, Zsolt. 2014. "The Discreet Charm of Political Parties." *Party Politics* 20:194–204.

Epstein, Leon. 1967. *Political Parties in Western Democracies*. London: Pall Mall.

Esaiasson, Peter, and Knut Heidar, eds. 2000. *Beyond Westminster and Congress: The Nordic Experience*. Columbus: Ohio State University Press.

Esaiasson, Peter, and Sören Holmberg. 1996. *Representation from Above. Members of Parliament and Representative Democracy in Sweden*. Aldershot: Dartmouth Publishing.

Ezrow, Lawrence, Catherine De Vries, Marco Steenbergen, and Erica Edwards. 2011. "Mean Voter Representation and Partisan Constituency Representation: Do Parties Respond to the Mean Voter Position or to Their Supporters?" *Party Politics* 17:275–301.

Falke, Wolfgang. 1982. *Die Mitglieder Der CDU: Eine Empirische Studie Zum Verhältnis von Mitglieder-Und Organisationsstruktur Der CDU 1971–1977*. Berlin: Duncker & Humblot.

Farrell, David M., and Paul Webb. 2000. "Political Parties as Campaign Organizations." In *Parties without Partisans*, edited by Russell J. Dalton and Martin P. Wattenberg, 102–28. Oxford: Oxford University Press.

Gallagher, Michael, Michael Laver, and Peter Mair. 2011. *Representative Government in Modern Europe*. 5th ed. London: McGraw-Hill Higher Education.

Gallagher, Michael, and Michael Marsh. 2002. *Days of Blue Loyalty: The Politics of Membership of the Fine Gael Party*. Dublin: PSAI Press.

———. 2004. "Party Membership in Ireland: The Members of Fine Gael." *Party Politics* 10:407–25.

Gauja, Anika. 2013a. *The Politics of Party Policy: From Members to Legislators*. Houndmills: Palgrave Macmillan.

———. 2013b. "Policy Development and Intra-Party Democracy." In *The Challenges of Intra-Party Democracy*, edited by William P. Cross and Richard S. Katz, 116–35. Oxford: Oxford University Press. http://www.oxfordscholarship.com/view/10.1093/acprof:oso/9780199661879.001.0001/acprof-9780199661879-chapter-8.

Golder, Matt, and Jacek Stramski. 2010. "Ideological Congruence and Electoral Institutions." *American Journal of Political Science* 54:90–106.

Green-Pedersen, Christoffer. 2007. "The Growing Importance of Issue Competition. The Changing Nature of Party Competition in Western Europe." *Political Studies* 55:608–28.

Greve, Tim. 1953. *Nominasjon ved Stortingsvalg*. Bergen: Christians Michelsens Institutt.

Gulbrandsen, Trygve, Fredrik Engelstad, Trond Beldo Klausen, Hege Skjeie, Mari Teigen, and Øyvind Østerud. 2002. *Norske makteliter*. Oslo: Gyldendal Akademisk.

van Haute, Emilie, and Anika Gauja, eds. 2015. *Party Members and Activists*. London: Routledge.

Hazan, Reuven Y., and Gideon Rahat. 2010. *Democracy within Parties: Candidate Selection Methods and Their Political Consequences*. Oxford: Oxford University Press.

Heidar, Knut. 1988. *Partidemokrati på prøve*. Oslo: Universitetsforlaget.

———. 1994. "The Polymorphic Nature of Party Membership." *European Journal of Political Research* 25:61–86.

———. 2000. "Parliamentary Party Groups." In *Beyond Westminster and Congress: The Nordic Experience,* edited by Peter Esaiasson and Knut Heidar, 183–209. Columbus: Ohio State University Press.

———. 2001. *Norway. Elites on Trial.* Boulder, CO: Westview Press.

———. 2005. "Norwegian Parties and the Party System: Steadfast and Changing." *West European Politics* 28:807–33.

———. 2006. "Party Membership and Participation." In *The Handbook of Party Politics,* edited by Richard S. Katz and William Crotty, 301–15. London: Sage.

———. 2013. *Stortingsundersøkelsen 2012. Rapport fra en surveystudie for historieprosjektet om Stortingets historie 1964–2014.* Oslo: Department of Political Science, University of Oslo.

———. 2014. "Partiene—fra aristokratiske diskusjonsklubber til populistiske meningsbyråer?" In *Det norske demokratiet i det 21. århundre,* edited by Harald Baldersheim and Øyvind Østerud, 157–75. Bergen: Fagbokforlaget.

———. 2015. "Party Membership in Norway: Declining, but Still Viable?" In *Party Members and Activists,* edited by Anika Gauja and Emilie van Haute. London: Routledge.

Heidar, Knut, and Ruud Koole. 2000. "Parliamentary Party Groups Compared." In *Parliamentary Party Groups in European Democracies: Political Parties behind Closed Doors,* edited by Knut Heidar and Ruud Koole, 248–70. London: Routledge.

Heidar, Knut, Karina Kosiara-Pedersen, and Jo Saglie. 2012. "Party Change and Party Member Participation in Denmark and Norway." In *Democracy, Elections and Political Parties,* edited by Jens Blom-Hansen, Christoffer Green-Pedersen, and Svend-Erik Skaaning, 155–63. Århus: Politica.

Heidar, Knut, and Jo Saglie. 2002. *Hva skjer med partiene?* Oslo: Gyldendal Norsk Forlag.

———. 2003a. "A Decline of Linkage? Intra-Party Participation in Norway, 1991–2000." *European Journal of Political Research* 42:761–86.

———. 2003b. "Predestined Parties? Organizational Change in Norwegian Political Parties." *Party Politics* 9:219–39.

Hellevik, Ottar. 1969. *Stortinget—en sosial elite?* Oslo: Pax.

Holmberg, Sören. 1974. *Riksdagen representerar svenska folket: empiriska studier i representativ demokrati.* Lund: Studentlitteratur.

———. 2000. "Issue Agreement." In *Beyond Westminster and Congress: The Nordic Experience,* edited by Peter Esaiasson and Knut Heidar, 155–80. Columbus: Ohio State University Press.

———. 2011. "Dynamic Representation from Above." In *How Democracy Works: Political Representation and Policy Congruence in Modern Societies,* edited by Bas Denters, Martin Rosema, and Kees Aarts, 53–76. Amsterdam: Amsterdam University Press.

Ignazi, Piero. 1996. "The Crisis of Parties and the Rise of New Political Parties." *Party Politics* 2:549–66.

———. 2014. "Power and the (Il)legitimacy of Political Parties: An Unavoidable Paradox of Contemporary Democracy?" *Party Politics* 20:160–69.

Jensen, Torben K. 2000. "Party Cohesion." In *Beyond Westminster and Congress: The Nordic Experience,* edited by Peter Esaiasson and Knut Heidar, 210–36. Columbus: Ohio State University Press.

Jupskås, Anders Ravik. 2009. *Rapport: Partimedlems- og landsmøtedelegatundersøkelsen 2009.* Oslo: Department of Political Science, University of Oslo.

———. 2015. "The Persistence of Populism. The Norwegian Progress Party 1973–2009." PhD diss., University of Oslo.

Karlsen, Rune. 2009. "Campaign Communication and the Internet. Party Strategy in the 2005 Norwegian Election Campaign." *Journal of Elections, Public Opinion & Parties* 19:183–202.

———. 2010. "Fear of the Political Consultant. Campaign Professionals and New Technology in Norwegian Electoral Politics." *Party Politics* 16:193–214.

———. 2013. "Obama's Online Success and European Party Organizations. Adoption and Adaptation of US Online Practices in the Norwegian Labor Party." *Journal of Information Technology and Politics* 10:158–70.

Karlsen, Rune, and Bernt Aardal. 2011. "Dagsorden og sakseierskap." In *Det politiske landskap. En studie av stortingsvalget i 2009,* edited by Bernt Aardal, 131–62. Oslo: Cappelen-Damm.

———. 2014. "Political Values Count but Issue Ownership Decides? How Stable and Dynamic Factors Influence Party Set and Vote Choice in Multiparty Systems." *International Political Science Review.* Published online before print November 26, 2014 doi:10.1177/0192512114558456.

———. 2015. "Politiske saker i valgkampen." In *Valg og velgere. En studie av stortingsvalget 2013,* edited by Bernt Aardal and Johannes Bergh, 34–48. Oslo: Cappelen-Damm.

Katz, Richard S. 1987. "Party Government and Its Alternatives." In *Party Governments: European and American Experiences,* edited by Richard S. Katz, 1–26. Berlin: de Gruyter.

———. 1990. "Party as Linkage: A Vestigial Function?" *European Journal of Political Research* 18:143–61.

———. 1997. *Democracy and Elections.* New York: Oxford University Press.

———. 2013. "Should We Believe That Improved Intra-Party Democracy Would Arrest Party Decline?" In *The Challenges of Intra-Party Democracy,* edited by William P. Cross and Richard S. Katz, 49–64. Oxford: Oxford University Press. http://www.oxfordscholarship.com/view/10.1093/acprof:oso/9780199661879.001.0001/acprof-9780199661879-chapter-4.

Katz, Richard S., and Peter Mair. 1995. "Changing Models of Party Organization and Party Democracy: The Emergence of the Cartel Party." *Party Politics* 1:5–28.

———. 2009. "The Cartel Party Thesis: A Restatement." *Perspectives on Politics* 7:753–66.

King, Anthony. 1969. "Political Parties in Western Democracies." *Polity* 2:111–41.

Kirchheimer, Otto. 1966. "The Transformation of the Western European Party Systems." In *Political Parties and Political Development,* edited by Joseph LaPalombara and Myron Weiner, 177–200. Princeton, NJ: Princeton University Press.

Kittilson, Miki Caul. 2013. "Party Politics." In *The Oxford Handbook of Gender and Politics,* edited by Georgina Waylen, Karen Celis, Johanna Kantola, and S. Laurel Weldon, 536–53. New York: Oxford University Press. http://www.oxfordhandbooks.com/view/10.1093/oxfordhb/9780199751457.001.0001/oxfordhb-9780199751457-e-21.

Knutsen, Oddbjørn. 2004. "Voters and Social Cleavages." In *Nordic Politics: Comparative Perspectives,* edited by Knut Heidar. Oslo: Universitetsforlaget.

Koss, Michael. 2011. *The Politics of Party Funding. State Funding to Political Parties and Party Competition in Western Europe.* Oxford: Oxford University Press.

Lawson, Kay, ed. 1980. *Political Parties and Linkages.* New Haven: Yale University Press.

Lawson, Kay, and Peter H. Merkl, eds. 1988. *When Parties Fail. Emerging Alternative Organizations.* Princeton: Princeton University Press.

Lijphart, Arend. 2013. *Patterns of Democracy: Government Forms and Performance in Thirty-Six Countries.* New Haven: Yale University Press.

Listhaug, Ola, and Hanne Marthe Narud. 2011. "The Changing Macro Context of Norwegian Voters: From Center-Periphery Cleavages to Oil Wealth." In *How Democracy Works: Political Representation and Policy Congruence in Modern Societies,* edited by Bas Denters, Martin Rosema, and Kees Aarts, 239–56. Amsterdam: Amsterdam University Press/Pallas Publications.

Loxbo, Karl. 2013. "The Fate of Intra-Party Democracy: Leadership Autonomy and Activist Influence in the Mass Party and the Cartel Party." *Party Politics* 19:537–54.

Luttbeg, Norman R. 1974. *Public Opinion and Public Policy: Models of Political Linkage.* 3rd ed. Ithaca, NY: F. E. Peacock.

Mackie, Thomas T., and Richard Rose. 1991. *The International Almanac of Electoral History.* 3rd ed. Washington, DC: Congressional Quarterly Inc.

Mair, Peter. 2006. "Ruling the Void: The Hollowing of Western Democracy." *The New Left Review* 42:25–51.

———. 2008. "The Challenge to Party Government." *West European Politics* 31:1–2, 211–34.

———. 2013. *Ruling the Void: The Hollowing of Western Democracy.* London: Verso.

Manin, Bernard. 1997. *The Principles of Representative Government.* Cambridge: Cambridge University Press.

Mansbridge, Jane. 1999. "Should Blacks Represent Blacks and Women Represent Women? A Contingent 'Yes.'" *Journal of Politics* 61:628–57.

Marien, Sofie, Marc Hooghe, and Ellen Quintelier. 2010. "Inequalities in Non-Institutionalised Forms of Political Participation: A Multi-Level Analysis of 25 Countries." *Political Studies* 58:187–213.

Matthews, Donald R., and Henry Valen. 1999. *Parliamentary Representation. The Case of the Norwegian Storting.* Columbus: Ohio State Press.

May, John D. 1973. "Opinion Structure of Political Parties: The Special Law of Curvilinear Disparity." *Political Studies* 21:135–51.

McKenzie, Robert. 1982. "Power in the Labour Party: The Issue of 'Intra-Party Democracy.'" In *The Politics of the Labour Party,* edited by Dennis Kavanagh. London: Allen and Unwin.

van der Meer, Tom W.G., and Erik J. van Ingen. 2009. "Schools of Democracy? Disentangling the Relationship between Civic Participation and Political Action in 17 European Countries." *European Journal of Political Research* 48:281–308.

Michels, Robert. (1911) 1962. *Political Parties: A Sociological Study of the Oligarchical Tendencies of Modern Democracies.* New York: Free Press.

Milbrath, Lester W. 1965. *Political Participation: How and Why Do People Get Involved in Politics?* Chicago: Rand McNally & Company.

Miller, David. 1983. "The Competitive Model of Democracy." In *Democratic Theory and Practice,* edited by Graeme Duncan, 133–55. Cambridge: Cambridge University Press.

Miller, Warren E., Roy Pierce, Jacques Thomassen, Richard Herrera, Sören Holmberg, Peter Esaiasson, and Bernhard Wessels. 1999. *Policy Representation in Western Democracies.* Oxford: Oxford University Press.

Miller, Warren, and Donald Stokes. 1963. "Constituency Influence in Congress." *American Political Science Review* 57:45–56.

Narud, Hanne Marthe. 2008. "Partienes nominasjoner. Hvem deltar? Og spiller det noen rolle?" *Tidsskrift for samfunnsforskning* 49:543–73.

———. 2011. "Politiske avstander og regjeringsalternativ ved valget i 2009." In *Det politiske landskap. En studie av stortingsvalget i 2009,* edited by Bernt Aardal, 195–224. Oslo: Cappelen-Damm.

Narud, Hanne Marthe, Bjørn Erik Rasch, and Henry Valen. 2005. *Stortingsundersøkelsen våren 2005. Spørreundersøkelse blant stortingsrepresentantene.* Oslo: Department of Political Science, University of Oslo.

Narud, Hanne Marthe, and Audun Skare. 1999. "Are Party Activists the Party Extremists? The Patterns of Opinions in Political Parties." *Scandinavian Political Studies* 22:45–65.

Narud, Hanne Marthe, and Henry Valen. 2000. "Does Background Matter? Social Representation and Political Attitudes." In *Beyond Westminster and Congress: The Nordic Experience,* edited by Peter Esaiasson and Knut Heidar, 83–106. Columbus: Ohio State University Press.

———. 2007a. "The Conditional Party Mandate: A Model for the Study of Mass and Elite Patterns." *European Journal of Political Research* 46:293–318.

———. 2007b. *Demokrati og ansvar. Om politisk representasjon i et flerpartisystem.* Oslo: Damm forlag.

———. 2008. "The Norwegian Storting: 'People's Parliament' or Coop for 'Political Broilers'?" *World Political Science Review* 4:1–34.

———. 2009. *The Funding of Party Competition. Political Finance in 25 Democracies.* Baden-Baden: Nomos.

Neumann, Sigmund. 1956. *Modern Political Parties: Approaches to Comparative Politics.* Chicago: University of Chicago Press.

Norris, Pippa. 1995. "May's Law of Curvilinear Disparity Revisited: Leaders, Officers, Members and Voters in British Political Parties." *Party Politics* 1:29–47.

———. 2011. *Democratic Deficit. Critical Citizens Revisited.* Oxford: Oxford University Press.

Ostrogorski, Mosei. 1902. *Democracy and the Organization of Political Parties.* 2 vols. London: Macmillan and Co. Limited. http://archive.org/details/democracyandtheo031734mbp.

Ot. prp. (parliamentary bill) no. 84. 2004–2005. *Om lov om visse forhold vedrørende de politiske partiene (partiloven)* [On the Law Concerning Certain Conditions Regarding Political Parties (the 'Party Law')].

Pedersen, Karina, Lars Bille, Roger Buch, Jørgen Elkit, Bernhard Hansen, and Hans Jørgen Nielsen. 2004. "Sleeping or Active Partners? Danish Party Members at the Turn of the Millennium." *Party Politics* 10:367–83.

Pedersen, Karina, and Jo Saglie. 2005. "New Technology in Ageing Parties. Internet Use in Danish and Norwegian Parties." *Party Politics* 11:359–77.

Pelizzo, Riccardo. 2003. "Cartel Parties and Cartel Party Systems." PhD diss., Johns Hopkins University.

Phillips, Anne. 1995. *The Politics of Presence.* Oxford: Oxford University Press.

Pierce, Roy. 1999. "Mass-Elite Issue Linkages and the Responsible Party Model of Representation." In *Policy Representation in Western Democracies,* edited by Warren Miller, Roy Pierce, Jacques Thomassen, Richard Herrera, Sören Holmberg, Peter Esaiasson, and Bernard Wessels, 9–32. Oxford: Oxford University Press.

Pierre, Jon, Lars Svåsand, and Anders Widfeldt. 2000. "State Subsidies to Political Parties: Confronting Rhetoric with Reality." *West European Politics* 23:1–24.

Pilet, Jean-Benoit, and William Cross, eds. 2014. *The Selection of Political Party Leaders in Contemporary Parliamentary Democracies: A Comparative Study.* London: Routledge.

Pitkin, Hanna Fenichel. 1967. *The Concept of Representation.* Berkeley: University of California Press.

Poguntke, Thomas. 2002. "Party Organization Linkage: Parties without Firm Social Roots?" In *Political Parties in the New Europe: Political and Analytical Challenges,* edited by Kurt Richard Luther and Ferdinand Müller-Rommel, 43–62. Oxford: Oxford University Press.

Poguntke, Thomas, and Paul Webb. 2005. *The Presidentialization of Politics. A Comparative Study of Modern Democracies.* Oxford: Oxford University Press.

Pomper, Gerald. 1992. "Concepts of Political Parties." *Journal of Theoretical Politics* 4:143–59.

Putnam, Robert. 1976. *The Comparative Study of Political Elites.* Englewood Cliffs, NJ: Prentice-Hall.

Rae, Douglas W., and H. Daudt. 1976. "The Ostrogorski Paradox: A Peculiarity of Compound Majority Decision." *European Journal of Political Research* 4:391–98.

Rahat, Gideon, Reuven Y. Hazan, and Richard S. Katz. 2008. "Democracy and Political Parties: On the Uneasy Relationships between Participation, Competition and Representation." *Party Politics* 14:663–83.

Ranney, Austin. 1951. "Toward a More Responsible Two-Party System: A Commentary." *The American Political Science Review* 45:488–99.

Robertson, David. 1976. *A Theory of Party Competition.* London: John Wiley and Sons.

Rohrschneider, Robert, and Stephen Whitefield. 2012. *The Strain of Representation. How Parties Represent Diverse Voters in Western and Eastern Europe.* Oxford: Oxford University Press.

Rokkan, Stein. 1967. "Geography, Religion, and Social Class: Crosscutting Cleavages in Norwegian Politics." In *Party Systems and Voter Alignments: Cross-National Perspectives,* edited by Seymour Martin Lipset and Stein Rokkan, 367–444. New York: Free Press.

Rommetvedt, Hilmar. 1991. "Partiavstand og partikoalisjoner." PhD diss., University of Bergen.

———. 2003. *The Rise of the Norwegian Parliament.* London: Frank Cass.

———. 2005. "Norway: Resources Count, but Votes Decide? From Neo-corporatist Representation to Neo-pluralist Parliamentarism." *West European Politics* 28:740–63.

Rose, Richard, ed. 1974. *Electoral Behaviour: A Comparative Handbook.* New York: Free Press.

Saglie, Jo, and Knut Heidar. 2004. "Democracy within Norwegian Political Parties. Complacency or Pressure for Change?" *Party Politics* 10:385–405.

Sartori, Giovanni. 1976. *Parties and Party Systems.* Cambridge: Cambridge University Press.

Scarrow, Susan E. (2000) 2002. "Parties without Members? Party Organization in a Changing Environment." In *Parties without Partisans,* edited by Russell J. Dalton and Martin P. Wattenberg, 79–101. Oxford: Oxford University Press.

———. 2002. "Introduction." In *Perspectives on Political Parties: Classic Readings,* edited by Susan E. Scarrow, 1–26. London: Palgrave.

———. 2006. "Party subsidies and the freezing of party competition: Do cartel mechanisms work?" *West European Politics* 29:619–39.

———. 2015. *Beyond Party Members: Changing Approaches to Partisan Mobilization.* Oxford: Oxford University Press.

Scarrow, Susan E., and Burcu Gezgor. 2010. "Declining Memberships, Changing Members? European Political Party Members in a New Era." *Party Politics* 16:823–43.

Schattschneider, E.E. 1942. *Party Government.* New York: Rinehart.

Schmitt, Herman, and Jacques Thomassen. 1999. *Political Representation and Legitimacy in the European Union.* Oxford: Oxford University Press.

Schumpeter, Joseph. 1942. *Capitalism, Socialism and Democracy.* New York: Harper & Row.

Spier, Tim, Markus Klein, Ulrich von Alemann, Hanna Hoffmann, Annika Laux, Alexandra Nonnenmacher, and Katharina Rohrbach, eds. 2011. *Parteimitglieder in Deutschland: Die Potsdamer Partei Mitgliederstudie.* Wiesbaden: VS Verlag.

Spies, Dennis C., and André Kaiser. 2014. "Does the Mode of Candidate Selection Affect the Representativeness of Parties?" *Party Politics* 20:576–90.

Stimson, James A., Michael B. Mackuen, and Robert S. Erikson. 1995. "Dynamic Representation." *American Political Science Review* 89:543–65.

Stokes, Susan C. 1999. "Political Parties and Democracy." *Annual Review of Political Science* 2:243–67.

Strøm, Kaare, Wolfgang C. Müller, and Torbjörn Bergman, eds. 2003. *Delegation and Accountability in Parliamentary Democracies*. Oxford: Oxford University Press.

Strøm, Kaare, and Hanne Marthe Narud. 2003. "Norway: Virtual Parliamentarism." In *Delegation and Accountability in Parliamentary Democracies*, edited by Kaare Strøm, Wolfgang C. Müller, and Torbjörn Bergman, 523–52. Oxford: Oxford University Press.

Strøm, Kaare and Lars Svåsand, eds. 1997. *Challenges to Political Parties: The Case of Norway*. Ann Arbor, MI: University of Michigan Press.

Sundberg, Jan. 1987. "Exploring the Basis of Declining Party Membership in Denmark: A Scandinavian Comparison." *Scandinavian Political Studies* 10:17–38.

Svåsand, Lars. 1992. "Norway." In *Party Organisations: A data handbook*, edited by Peter Mair and Richard Katz, 732–80. London: Sage.

———. 1994a. "Change and Adaptation in Norwegian Party Organizations." In *How Parties Organize: Change and Adaptation in Party Organizations in Western Democracies*, edited by Peter Mair and Richard S. Katz, 304–31. London: Sage.

———. 1994b. "Fra mangfold til standardisering: Om utformingen av partienes organisasjoner." In *Partiene i en brytningstid*, edited by Knut Heidar and Lars Svåsand, 104–24. Bergen: Alma Mater Forlag.

———. 1994c. "Partienes finansieringsmønster: fra medlemmenes lommebøker til statsbudsjettet." In *Partiene i en brytningstid*, edited by Knut Heidar and Lars Svåsand, 180–212. Bergen: Alma Mater Forlag.

Thomassen, Jacques. 1994. "Empirical Research into Political Representation: Failing Democracy or Failing Models?" In *Elections at Home and Abroad*, edited by M. Kent Jennings and Thomas E. Mann, 237–64. Michigan: Michigan University Press.

———. 2012. "The Blind Corner of Political Representation." *Representation* 48:13–27.

Thomassen, Jacques, and Carolien van Ham. 2014. "Failing Political Representation or a Change in Kind? Models of Representation and Empirical Trends in Europe." *West European Politics* 37:400–19.

Thomassen, Jacques, and Hermann Schmitt. 1999. "Issue Congruence." In *Political Representation and Legitimacy in the European Union*, edited by Hermann Schmitt and Jacques Thomassen, 186–208. Oxford: Oxford University Press.

Valen, Henry. 1954. "Nominasjon av stortingskandidater i Det norske Arbeiderparti." Master's thesis, University of Oslo.

———. 1958. "Factional Activities and Nominations in Political Parties." *Acta Sociologica* 3:183–99.

———. 1966. "The Recruitment of Parliamentary Nominees in Norway." *Scandinavian Political Studies* 1:121–66.

———. 1988. "Norway: Decentralization and Group Representation." In *Candidate Selection in Comparative Perspective: The Secret Garden of Politics*, edited by Michael Gallagher and Michael Marsh, 210–35. London: Sage.

Valen, Henry, and Bernt Aardal. 1994. "The Norwegian Programme of Electoral Research." *European Journal of Political Research* 25:287–309.

Valen, Henry, Hanne Marthe Narud, and Audun Skare. 2002. "Norway: Party Dominance and Decentralized Decision-Making." In *Party Sovereignty and Citizen Control: Selecting*

Candidates for Parliamentary Elections in Denmark, Finland, Iceland and Norway, edited by Hanne Marthe Narud, Mogens N. Pedersen, and Henry Valen, 169–215. Odense: University Press of Southern Denmark.

Valen, Henry, and Stein Rokkan. 1974. "Norway: Conflict Structure and Mass Politics in a European Periphery." In *Electoral Behavior: A Comparative Handbook,* edited by Richard Rose. New York: Free Press.

Verba, Sidney, Norman Nie, and Jae-on Kim. 1978. *Participation and Political Equality.* Cambridge: Cambridge University Press.

Voerman, Gerrit and Wijbrandt van Schuur. 2011. "Dutch Political Parties and Their Members." In *Party Membership in Europe: Exploration into the Anthills of Party Politics,* edited by Emilie van Haute. Bruzelles: Editions de Université de Bruxelles.

Volkens, Andrea, and Hans-Dieter Klingemann. 2002. "Parties, Ideologies, and Issues: Stability and Change in Fifteen European Party Systems 1945–1998." In *Political Parties in the New Europe: Political and Analytical Challenges,* edited by Kurt Richard Luther and Ferdinand Müller-Rommel, 143–67. Oxford: Oxford University Press.

Ware, Alan. 1979. *The Logic of Party Democracy.* London: Macmillan.

Webb, Paul. 2000. "Political Parties in Western Europe: Linkage. Legitimacy and Reform." *Representation* 37:203–14.

Whiteley, Paul. 2009. "Party Membership and Activism in Comparative Perspective." In *Activating the Citizen. Dilemmas of Participation in Europe and Canada,* edited by Joan DeBardeleben and Jon H. Pammett, 131–51. Basingstoke, UK: Palgrave Macmillan. http://repository.essex.ac.uk/8228/.

———. 2011. "Is the Party Over? The Decline of Party Activism and Membership across the Democratic World." *Party Politics* 17:21–44.

Whiteley, Paul, and Patrick Seyd. 1998. "The Dynamics of Party Activism in Britain: A Spiral of Demobilization?" *The British Journal of Political Science* 28:113–37.

———. 2002. *High-Intensity Participation: The Dynamics of Party Activism in Britain.* Ann Arbor: University of Michigan Press.

Whiteley, Paul, Patrick Seyd, and Jeremy Richardson. 1994. *True Blues: The Politics of Conservative Party Membership.* Oxford: Oxford University Press.

Widfeldt, Anders. 1995. "Party Membership and Party Representativeness." In *Citizens and the State,* edited by Hans-Dieter Klingemann and Dieter Fuchs, 134–80. Oxford: Oxford University Press.

———. 1999a. *Linking Parties with People?: Party Membership in Sweden 1960–1997.* Aldershot: Ashgate.

———. 1999b. "Losing Touch? The Political Representativeness of Swedish Parties, 1985–1994." *Scandinavian Political Studies* 22:307–26.

Wright, William. 1971. "Comparative Party Models: Rational-Efficient and Party Democracy." In *A Comparative Study of Party Organization,* edited by William Wright, 17–54. Columbus: Merrill.

Young, Lisa. 2013. "Party Members and Intra-Party Democracy." In *The Challenges of Intra-Party Democracy,* edited by William P. Cross and Richard S. Katz, 65–80. Oxford: Oxford University Press. http://www.oxfordscholarship.com/view/10.1093/acprof:oso/9780199661879.001.0001/acprof-9780199661879-chapter-5.

Index

activism, 23–24; decline, 26, 57
activists, 7, 15, 16, 29, 120, 121; curvilinear
    law and, 14; mid-level, 2, 4, 17, 47,
    125, 126
age congruence, in Norway, 74, 79–81, 87,
    122; by party, 80, *81*, *89–90*; percentage
    shares, *80*, *88–90*
Agree index (AI), of Holmberg, 102, 105,
    106, 116n6
Ap. *See* Labour Party

bottom-up influence processes, 18, 19, 20;
    membership activity and representative
    capacity, 23–27; in Norway, 46, 47, 55
Burke, Edmund, 12, 21n1

candidates: party representation, 12;
    selection, 5, 10, 15, 17, 20, 31, 36;
    social composition and, 16–17
candidate selection and party discipline,
    in Norway, 50, 120; closed party
    conventions, 2, 44; new selection
    criteria, 45; Nomination Act of 1920,
    45; PR in elections, 44
cartel party, 3, 15, 33, 119
catch-all party, of Kirchheimer, 3, 32
Centre Party (Sp), in Norway, 36, 37, 50,
    53n3; membership percentage decrease,

41, 57, *58*, 74; member statutes, 46;
    voters and MPs policy congruence, 117n7
Christian People's Party (KrF), in Norway,
    36, 50; membership percentage decrease,
    41, 57, *58*, 74; member statutes, 46;
    policies, 37
closed party conventions, in Norway, 2, 44
CoAr. *See* common area under the graphs
Coastal Party, in Norway, 53n5
common area under the graphs (CoAr)
    measurement, 101, *101*, 102, 103, 105,
    106, 116n6
communication. *See* party communication
Comparative Study of Electoral Systems, 31
competition. *See* electoral competition *vs.*
    organized linkage; party competition
Conservatives (H), in Norway, 36, 50; least
    finance dependence, 44; membership
    percentage decrease, 41, 57, *58*, 74;
    member statutes, 46; on party subsidies,
    54n14; tax and educational policies, 38
curvilinear law of relationship, of May, 14,
    17, 100, 124

data material in study, of Norway, 38,
    48–50, *49*, 54n20
decision-making process, 6, 26; in
    Duverger's mass party model, 56;

141

About the Authors

Elin Haugsgjerd Allern is professor of political science at the University of Oslo. She has published on issues related to parties as organizations, the relationship between parties and interest groups, and political parties and government. She is the author of *Political Parties and Interest Groups in Norway* (ECPR Press, 2010) and guest editor of a special issue of *Party Politics* on party-interest group relationships (with Tim Bale, 2012).

Knut Heidar is professor of political science at the University of Oslo. He studied at Brandeis University and London School of Economics and Political Science. He is the author of books on Norwegian and West European politics, particularly focusing on parties and parliaments. He has published widely on comparative party research since the 1970s.

Rune Karlsen is research professor at the Institute for Social Research in Oslo. He has published widely on topics related to political communication, political parties, and election campaigns.

Lightning Source UK Ltd.
Milton Keynes UK
UKOW02n0747051215

264116UK00001B/26/P

9 781498 516549